Series 63
Uniform Securities Agent State Law Exam

License Exam Manual

2nd Edition

KAPLAN FINANCIAL

At press time, this edition contains the most complete and accurate information currently available. Owing to the nature of license examinations, however, information may have been added recently to the actual test that does not appear in this edition. Please contact the publisher to verify that you have the most current edition.

This publication is designed to provide accurate and authoritative information in regard to the subject matter covered. It is sold with the understanding that the publisher is not engaged in rendering legal, accounting, or other professional services. If legal advice or other expert assistance is required, the services of a competent professional should be sought.

We value your input and suggestions. If you found imperfections in this product, please let us know by sending an email to **errata@kaplan.com**. Please include the title, edition, and PPN (reorder number) of the material.

We are always looking for ways to make our products better to help you achieve your career goals.

SERIES 63 UNIFORM SECURITIES AGENT STATE LAW EXAM, 2ND EDITION
©2006, 2007 DF Institute, Inc. All rights reserved.

Published by DF Institute, Inc.

Printed in the United States of America.

ISBN: 1-4277-5804-2

PPN: 3663-0123

07	08	10	9	8	7	6	5	4	3	2	1
J	F	**M**	A	M	J	J	A	S	O	N	D

Contents

Hotsheets   159

Series 63 Introduction

INTRODUCTION

Thank you for choosing this exam preparation system for your educational needs and welcome to the Series 63 License Exam Manual. This manual has applied adult learning principles to give you the tools you'll need to pass your exam on the first attempt.

Some of these special features include:

■ exam-focused questions and content to maximize exam preparation;

■ an interactive design that integrates content with questions to increase retention; and

■ integrated Drill & Practice exam preparation tools to sharpen test-taking skills.

Why Do I Need to Pass the Series 63 Exam?

State securities laws require individuals to pass a qualification exam to sell securities within their states. Almost all states require individuals to pass the Series 63 exam as a condition of state registration.

Are There Any Prerequisites?

Although there are no prerequisites for Series 63, some states require you to pass an NASD exam, which is a corequisite exam that must be completed in addition to the Series 63 before a individual can become registered with a state. You may take either exam first but must complete both satisfactorily.

What Is the Series 63 Exam Like?

The Uniform Securities Agent Law Examination consists of 65 multiple-choice questions. Applicants are allowed 75 minutes to complete the test. Of the 65 questions on the exam, 60 will count toward the final score. The remaining 5 questions are being tested for possible inclusion in the test bank for future use. These questions may appear anywhere in the exam and are not identified.

What Score Must I Achieve to Pass?

You need a score of at least 70% on the Series 63 exam to pass and become eligible for registration as a Securities Agent.

What Topics Will I See on the Exam?

The questions you will see on the Series 63 exam do not appear in any particular order. The computer is programmed to select a new, random set of questions for each exam taker, selecting questions according to the preset topic weighting of the exam. Each Series 63 candidate will see the same number of questions on each topic, but a different mix of questions. The Series 63 exam is divided into 4 critical function areas:

	# of Questions	% of Exam
Registration of Persons	18	30%
Securities	15	25%
Business Practices	21	35%
Administrative Provisions & Other Remedies	6	10%

When you complete your exam, you will receive a printout that identifies your performance in each area.

PREPARING FOR THE EXAM

How Is the License Exam Manual Organized?

The License Exam Manual consists of Units and Unit Tests organized to explain the material that NASAA has outlined for the exam. In addition to the regular text, each Unit also has some unique features designed to help with quick understanding of the material. When an additional point will be valuable to your comprehension, special notes are embedded in the text. Examples of these are included below.

TAKE NOTE   These highlight special or unusual information and amplify important points.

TEST TOPIC ALERT   Each Test Topic Alert! highlights content that is likely to appear on the exam.

EXAMPLE   These give practical examples and numerical instances of the material just covered and convert theory into practice.

You will also see Quick Quizzes, which will help ensure you understand and retain the material covered in that particular section. Quick Quizzes are a quick interactive review of what you just read.

Answers and rationale for the Quick Quizzes can be found at the end of each Unit.

In addition, HotSheets for each Unit summarize the key points in bullet-point format. For your convenience and use as review notes, these HotSheets are located at the end of the book on perforated pages.

If your study packet included a Drill & Practice CD-ROM, this CD includes a large bank of questions that are similar in style and content to those you will encounter on the exam. You may use it to generate tests by a specific topic or create exams that are similar in difficulty and proportionate mixture to the exam.

If you prefer to complete written tests, the Practice Final Tests will provide similar practice. The questions on the print tests are included in the CD. Devote a significant amount of your study time to the completion of practice questions and review of rationales on the CD and/or the Practice Final Tests.

Your study packet may also include Mastery Exams.

These are designed to closely simulate the true exam center experience in degree of difficulty and topic coverage and are an exceptional indicator of future actual exam score as well as areas of strength and weakness. When you have completed these exams, you will receive a detailed breakdown by topic of performance. This diagnostic breakdown will alert you to precisely where you need to concentrate further exam practice.

What Topics Are Covered in the Course?

The License Exam Manual consists of 4 Units, each devoted to a particular area of study that you will need to know to pass the Series 63. Each Unit is divided into study sections devoted to more specific areas with which you need to become familiar.

The Series 63 License Exam Manual addresses the following topics:

Unit	Topic
1	Registration of Persons
2	Securities
3	Business Practices
4	Administrative Provisions and Other Remedies

How Much Time Should I Spend Studying?

Plan to spend approximately 20–30 hours reading the material and carefully answering the questions. Spread your study time over the 2–3 weeks before the date on which you are scheduled to take the Series 63 exam. Your actual time may vary depending on your reading rate, comprehension, professional background, and study environment.

What Is the Best Way to Structure My Study Time?

The following schedule is suggested to help you obtain maximum retention from your study efforts. Remember, this is a guideline only, because each individual may require more or less time to complete the steps included.

Step 1. Read a Unit and complete the Unit Test. Review rationales for all questions whether you got them right or wrong (2–3 hours per Unit). In those instances where reference is made to an Appendix, please study it thoroughly.

Step 2. On the Drill & Practice CD-ROM, create and complete a test for each topic included under that Unit heading. For best results, select the maximum number of questions within each topic. Carefully review all rationales. Do an additional test on any topic on which you score under 60%. After completion of all topic tests, create a 60-question test comprising all Unit topics. Repeat this 60-question test until you score at least 70% (5–10 hours).

TAKE NOTE   Do not be overly concerned with your score on the first attempt at any of these tests. Instead, take the opportunity to learn from your mistakes and increase your knowledge.

Step 3. When you have completed all the Units and their Unit Tests, on the Drill & Practice CD-ROM, complete at least 5 of the 60-question exams. Complete as many as necessary to achieve a score of at least 80–90%. Create and complete additional topic tests as necessary to correct problem areas (10–20 hours).

Step 4. Each Mastery Exam mirrors the actual test in number of questions and subject matter coverage. Questions included in Mastery Exams are unique from all other question bank products, so you will see only new questions. Like the actual exam, you will not see the answer key and rationale, but the detailed diagnostic breakdown will provide you with clear guidance on areas where further study is required (2–3 hours per Exam).

Do I Need to Take All of the Practice Final Tests?

The Practice Final Tests assess the knowledge you need to answer the questions on the exam. By completing the Practice Final Tests and checking your answers against the rationales, you should be able to pinpoint areas of difficulty. Review any questions you miss, paying particular attention to their rationale. If any subjects still seem troublesome, go back and review the section(s) covering those topics.

How Well Can I Expect to Do?

The exams prepared by NASAA are not easy. You must display considerable understanding and knowledge of the topics presented in this course to pass the exam and qualify for registration.

If you study diligently, complete all sections of the course, and consistently score at least 85% on the tests, you should be well prepared to pass the exam. However, it is important for you to realize that merely knowing the answers to our questions will not enable you to pass unless you understand the essence of the information behind the question.

SUCCESSFUL TEST-TAKING TIPS

Passing the exam depends not only on how well you learn the subject matter, but also on how well you take exams. You can develop your test-taking skills—and improve your score—by learning a few test-taking techniques:

- Read the full question

- Avoid jumping to conclusions—watch for hedge clauses

- Interpret the unfamiliar question

- Look for key words and phrases

- Identify the intent of the question

- Memorize key points

- Avoid changing answers

- Pace yourself

Each of these pointers is explained below, including examples that show how to use them to improve your performance on the exam.

Read the Full Question

You cannot expect to answer a question correctly if you do not know what it is asking. If you see a question that seems familiar and easy, you might anticipate the answer, mark it, and move on before you finish reading it. This is a serious mistake. Be sure to read the full question before answering it—questions are often written to trap people who assume too much.

Avoid Jumping to Conclusions—Watch for Hedge Clauses

The questions on NASAA exams are often embellished with deceptive distractors as choices. To avoid being misled by seemingly obvious answers, make it a practice to read each question and each answer twice before selecting your choice. Doing so will provide you with a much better chance of doing well on the exam.

Watch out for hedge clauses embedded in the question. (Examples of hedge clauses include the terms *if, not, all, none,* and *except.*) In the case of *if* statements, the question can be answered correctly only by taking into account the qualifier. If you ignore the qualifier, you will not answer correctly.

Qualifiers are sometimes combined in a question. Some that you will frequently see together are *all* with *except* and *none* with *except*. In general, when a question starts with *all* or *none* and ends with *except*, you are looking for an answer that is opposite to what the question appears to be asking.

Interpret the Unfamiliar Question

Do not be surprised if some questions on the exam seem unfamiliar at first. If you have studied your material, you will have the information to answer all the questions correctly. The challenge may be a matter of understanding what the question is asking.

Very often, questions present information indirectly. You may have to interpret the meaning of certain elements before you can answer the question. Be aware that the exam will approach a concept from different angles.

Look for Key Words and Phrases

Look for words that are tip-offs to the situation presented. For example, if you see the word *prospectus* in the question, you know the question is about a new issue. Sometimes a question will even supply you with the answer if you can recognize the key words it contains. Few questions provide blatant clues, but many do offer key words that can guide you to selecting the correct answer if you pay attention. Be sure to read all instructional phrases carefully.

Take time to identify the key words to answer this type of question correctly.

Identify the Intent of the Question

Many questions on NASAA exams supply so much information that you lose track of what is being asked. This is often the case in story problems. Learn to separate the story from the question.

Take the time to identify what the question is asking. Of course, your ability to do so assumes you have studied sufficiently. There is no method for correctly answering questions if you don't know the material.

Memorize Key Points

Reasoning and logic will help you answer many questions, but you will have to memorize a good deal of information. The HotSheets summarize some of the most important key points for memorization.

Avoid Changing Answers

If you are unsure of an answer, your first hunch is the one most likely to be correct. Do not change answers on the exam without good reason. In general, change an answer only if you:

■ discover that you did not read the question correctly; or

■ find new or additional helpful information in another question.

Pace Yourself

Some people will finish the exam early and some do not have time to finish all the questions. Watch the time carefully (your time remaining will be displayed on your computer screen) and pace yourself through the exam.

Do not waste time by dwelling on a question if you simply do not know the answer. Make the best guess you can, mark the question for *Record for Review*, and return to the question if time allows. Make sure that you have time to read all the questions so that you can record the answers you do know.

THE EXAM

How Do I Enroll in the Exam?

To obtain an admission ticket to a NASAA exam, your firm must file an application form and processing fees with the NASD. To take the exam, you should make an appointment with a Prometric Testing Center as far in advance as possible of the date on which you would like to take the exam.

You may schedule your appointment at Prometric, 24 hours a day, 7 days a week, on the Prometric secure Website at **www.prometric.com**. You may also use this site to reschedule or cancel your exam, locate a test center, and get a printed confirmation of your appointment. To speak with a Prometric representative by phone, please contact the Prometric Contact Center at 1-800-578-6273.

What Should I Take to the Exam?

Take one form of personal identification with your signature and photograph as issued by a government agency. You cannot take reference materials or anything else into the testing area. Calculators are available upon request. Scratch paper and pencils will be provided by the testing center, although you cannot take them with you when you leave.

Exam Results and Reports

At the end of the exam, your score will be displayed, indicating whether you passed. The next business day after your exam, your results will be mailed to your firm and to the self-regulatory organization and state securities commission specified on your application.

Periodically, new editions of this License Exam Manual are published to reflect improvements, regulatory changes, and modifications to testable content. Kaplan Financial publishes *TestAlerts!* to update existing editions with changes that have been incorporated in new editions. The *TestAlerts!* are available at no charge at **www.kaplanfinancial.com**. Click on *View Securities TestAlerts!* to access them.

We encourage you to check this Website before taking your exam to be sure you have the latest testable information.

After you review the *TestAlert!*, you may wish to upgrade to the next edition, but keep in mind that any new material and major changes will be found in the *TestAlert!*.

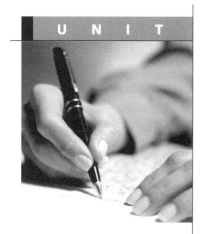

1

Registration of Persons

The Uniform Securities Act (USA) is model legislation designed to guide each state in drafting its state securities law. Questions on your Series 63 exam will be based on the latest version of the USA endorsed by the North American Securities Administrators Association (NASAA) as well as NASAA's statements of policy (Appendix A and B).

In 1996, the US Congress enacted the National Securities Markets Improvements Act (NSMIA), national legislation designed to integrate securities markets and eliminate conflicting state and federal securities legislation. The definitions and regulations contained in this license exam manual reflect the changes to the USA required by the NSMIA. After you finish this manual, carefully review the study guide in Appendix C, which contains a summary of the most important provisions of the USA.

To begin the study of the USA, you must understand the various persons and entities that engage in securities transactions. You must understand the distinctions between the four classes of persons subject to the USA, as defined in this Unit and their registration requirements. The term *person*, as used in the USA, refers to individual natural persons, such as agents and investment adviser representatives, and also to legal entities, such as broker/dealers and investment advisory firms.

The Series 63 exam will include 18 questions on the material presented in this Unit. ■

When you have completed this Unit, you should be able to:

- **identify** what is and what is not considered a *person*;

- **describe** the differences between exclusions from definitions and exemptions from provisions of the USA;

- **describe** the differences between broker/dealer, agent, investment adviser, and investment adviser representative;

- **recognize** the difference between a federal covered and a state registered investment adviser; and

- **identify,** for each category of professional, the procedures and requirements for registration in a state.

DEFINITION OF PERSON IN SECURITIES LAW

In securities legislation, such as the USA, terms that you are familiar with in normal speech have slightly different meanings under the law. The term *person* is one such example. Under the USA, person is used to refer to:

■ an individual human being or natural person; or

■ a legal person, such as a corporation or partnership.

A **natural person** means an individual person (human being) as the term is used in common, nonlegal conversation. Individual human beings subject to the act are agents and investment adviser representatives.

Legal persons (legal entities) are creatures of law. For example, a corporation or partnership is formed under the provisions of state law and therefore is a creature of law. For a legal entity to be sued in court, it must have legal existence or legal identity.

Legal entities, such as broker/dealers or investment advisory partnerships, can conduct business, commit criminal acts, bear civil liabilities, and be sued in court. They are legal persons subject to the USA. In the context of securities regulation, natural persons (individual agents) work for legal persons, such as broker/dealers and investment advisory firms.

TAKE NOTE

There are other legal persons included in the USA's definition of person, such as trusts, associations, joint-stock companies, governments, and political subdivisions of governments.

TEST TOPIC ALERT

Although there is a wide variety of entities that may be defined as persons, on the exam, there are only three nonpersons. They are:

■ minors (anyone unable to enter into contracts under the laws of the state);

■ deceased individuals; and

■ individuals legally declared mentally incompetent.

EXCLUSION FROM DEFINITIONS AND EXEMPTION FROM REGISTRATION

Understanding terms is not a mere semantic exercise. Definitions create jurisdiction. Jurisdiction means that a person or security is covered or subject to the law. Exemptions and exclusions affect persons covered by the act but provide for exemptions and exclusions from provisions of the act. These distinctions must be kept in mind.

Exclusion from a Definition

Exclusion means excluded from, or not included in, a definition. For the purposes of the USA, if a person is excluded from the definition of agent, that person is not subject to provisions of state law that refer to agents. An agent, which will be more fully defined later in this Unit, is any individual other than a broker/dealer who represents a broker/dealer or issuer in effecting transactions in securities.

There are, however, situations in which a person who is representing an issuer in securities transactions is not, by definition, an agent for purposes of the USA. How is this accomplished? By excluding that person from the definition. Here is what the act says:

Agent does not include an individual who represents an issuer in . . . (1) effecting transactions in a security exempted by [the act] . . . or . . . (2) effecting transactions exempted [by the act] or (3) effecting transactions with existing employees, partners, or directors of the issuer if no commission or other remuneration is paid or given directly or indirectly for soliciting any person in this state.

This means when a person performs the functions of an agent for an issuer (effecting transactions in securities on behalf of a company issuing shares to the public), that person is not defined as an agent by the act in three specific circumstances: (1) when effecting transactions in securities exempt from registration; (2) in transactions that are exempt from registration; and (3) when effecting transactions with existing employees, when no commissions are paid.

TAKE NOTE

Keep in mind that an individual who works for an issuer of securities is excluded from the definition of agent when engaging in transactions involving the issuer's securities, provided that the individual is not compensated for such participation by commissions or other remuneration based either directly or indirectly on the amount of securities sold. In other words, salaried employees engaged in distributing their employers' shares as part of an employee benefit plan would not be required to register as agents because they are by definition excluded from the definition. If such employees were compensated on the basis of the number of shares sold, they would be defined as agents and therefore would be subject to registration.

Exemption from Registration Under the Act

Exemption in the USA means not being subject to a registration provision of the act even though that person is otherwise covered by the act. For example, a person defined as an agent can be exempt from registration requirements as an agent because that person enjoys an exemption from registration under federal law.

When federal law, such as the Securities Act of 1933, exempts a person or security from registration, the individual states cannot then require that person or security to register under state law. Such person or security is **exempt**. The same logic holds true for exclusion. If a person is excluded from a definition under federal securities law, the states cannot then include that person in the definition to subject that person to state law. Such person or security is excluded.

The logic here should be obvious: if the separate states could require persons that are exempt from registration under federal law to register under state law, state laws would be in conflict with federal securities laws. The NSMIA was enacted to eliminate such conflicts between state and federal securities regulations. (The implications of the NSMIA on investment advisers will be further addressed later in this Unit, and on securities in Unit 2.)

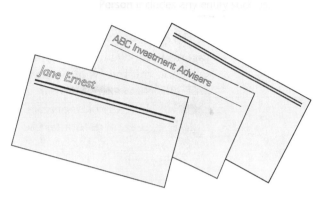

Individual or Business or Government

QUICK QUIZ 1.1

True or False?

F 1. A corporation is not a person; therefore, the state Administrator does not have jurisdiction over its securities activities.

F 2. An individual is a natural person and not a legal person subject to the jurisdiction of the USA.

Quick Quiz answers can be found at the end of the Unit.

PERSONS SUBJECT TO STATE REGISTRATION

Now that the terms *exclusion from a definition* and *exemption from registration* have been addressed, attention must now be directed to persons who are not excluded or exempted from provisions of the act. The following four classes of persons are included under the jurisdiction of state securities laws:

- Broker/dealers (generally legal persons such as corporations or partnerships)
- Agents (always individuals)
- Investment advisers (generally legal persons such as corporations or partnerships)
- Investment adviser representatives (always individuals)

TEST TOPIC ALERT

On your exam, always keep in mind which of the four categories of persons is the subject of the question. Rules that apply to agents, for example, are not the same as those that apply to broker/dealers. You will be tested on your understanding of the distinctions between each class of person defined in this Unit.

BROKER/DEALER

A **broker/dealer** is defined in the USA as any person (legal entity) engaged in the business of effecting transactions in securities for the accounts of others or for its own account. Any legal person (e.g., a securities firm) with an established place of business (an office) in the state that is in the business of buying and selling securities for the accounts of others (customers) and/or for its own proprietary account is a broker/dealer and must register in the state as such.

In other words, broker/dealers are firms for which registered representatives (agents) work. They are firms that engage in securities transactions, such as sales and trading. When acting on behalf of their customers—that is, buying and selling securities for their clients' accounts—broker/dealers act in an agency capacity. When broker/dealers buy and sell securities for their own accounts, called proprietary accounts, they act in a principal capacity as dealers.

TAKE NOTE   Individuals who buy and sell securities for their own accounts are not broker/dealers because they are engaged in personal investment activity, not the business of buying and selling securities for others. They are individual investors, not securities dealers.

Exclusions from the Definition of Broker/Dealer

Broker/dealers are firms that buy and sell securities for others or themselves as a business. There are, however, many persons, legal and natural, that effect securities transactions that are excluded from the definition of broker/dealer for purposes of state regulation. Persons not included in the definition of broker/dealer are:

- agents;

- issuers; and

- banks, savings institutions, and trust companies (not engaged in broker/dealer activities).

Domestic commercial banks and other financial institutions are generally excluded from the definition of broker/dealer. However, with the adoption of the Gramm-Leach-Bliley Act in 1999, also known as the Financial Modernization Act, federal securities law adopted a functional approach to the regulation of financial institutions. Under the functional approach, financial institutions that engage in brokerage-related securities activities are subject to SEC registration as broker/dealers as well as to applicable provisions of state securities law—the USA—that relate to broker/dealers.

Today, most banks and other financial institutions engage in securities activities through broker/dealer subsidiaries. The broker/dealer subsidiaries of banks are, as a result, not excluded from the definition of a broker/dealer and therefore subject to the same securities regulations as other broker/dealers. Keep in mind that formation of these subsidiaries eliminates the need for the bank holding companies to register as broker/dealers. Their broker/dealer subsidiaries must, of course, register.

Keep in mind the distinction between a bank holding company and a wholly owned commercial bank subsidiary. Commercial banks, the subsidiaries of bank holding companies, do not have to register because they are exempt. When engaged in securities transactions with the public, bank subsidiaries are subject to securities legislation as any other broker/dealer.

No Place of Business in the State

There is another exclusion from the definition of broker/dealer. This exclusion relates to the location of the broker/dealer's place of business. States exclude from the definition of broker/dealer those broker/dealers that:

- have no place of business in the state and deal exclusively with issuers, other broker/dealers, and other financial institutions, such as banks, savings and loan associations, trust companies, insurance companies, investment companies, and pension or profit-sharing trusts; and

- have no place of business in the state, but are licensed in a state where they have a place of business, and offer and sell securities in the state only with persons in the state who are existing customers and who are not residents of the state. This is sometimes referred to as the *snowbird* exemption.

In other words, the USA excludes broker/dealers with no place of business in the state from the definition of a broker/dealer to allow firms that deal exclusively with other financial institutions to operate in the state without registering. The reason for this exclusion is that broker/dealers who transact business solely with financial institutions are already subject to securities regulations by their functional regulators. Duplicate regulation is thereby eliminated.

The USA also allows broker/dealers to do business with existing customers who are temporarily in a state to avoid unnecessary multiple registrations. In most states, when an existing client legally changes residence to another state in which the broker/dealer is not registered, the firm has 30 days during which it may continue to do business with that client without registration in the new state. Should it wish to continue to maintain that client, the broker/dealer would have to register in that state.

Notice how important language is here: if broker/dealers with no place of business in the state were defined as broker/dealers, they would be subject to state registration. If such broker/dealers with no place of business in the state are not defined as broker/dealers, however, those broker/dealers are not subject to the registration requirements of that state. Language and definitions determine jurisdiction. If a person or entity is defined as a broker/dealer, that person is covered by (subject to) the provisions of the act. If a person or entity is excluded from a definition, that person is not subject to (covered by) the act.

The exam focuses more on the exclusions from the definition of broker/dealer than on the definition itself. Know these exclusions well.

Exclusion from the Definition of Broker/Dealer

Situation: First Securities Corporation is a registered broker/dealer with offices in Illinois. Mr. Thompson, an agent in the Illinois office of First Securities, recommends the purchase of ABC Shoes stock to his customer, Mr. Bixby, an Illinois resident, who is temporarily on vacation in Hawaii. Mr. Bixby agrees to the purchase of ABC Shoes, as well as other securities, while in Hawaii.

The Hawaiian state securities Administrator does not issue a cease and desist order against First Securities for unlawfully selling securities as an unregistered broker/dealer in Hawaii.

Analysis: The Hawaiian securities Administrator acted correctly by not issuing a cease and desist order against First Securities. Under the USA, First Securities is not required to register as a broker/dealer in Hawaii because it limits its business to an existing customer, Mr. Bixby, who is temporarily in the state. Because First Securities is properly registered in Illinois, it need not register in Hawaii, provided, of course, Mr. Bixby does not take up permanent residence there. In this case, First Securities does not fall under the definition of broker/dealer in Hawaii because it does not do business in Hawaii other than with one existing customer temporarily in the state. In this situation, First Securities is not defined as a broker/dealer in the state of Hawaii and therefore does not have to register as a broker/dealer in Hawaii. Definitions determine jurisdiction.

T A K E N O T E

A broker/dealer registered in Canada that does not have a place of business in this state is permitted to effect transactions in securities with a client from Canada who now lives in this state if those transactions are in a self-directed, tax-advantaged retirement plan (similar to an IRA) of which the individual client is the holder or contributor in Canada.

Broker/Dealer Registration Requirements

Under the USA, if a person is included in the definition of broker/dealer, that person must register as a broker/dealer in the states where it does business. The USA is clear about broker/dealer registration. It states, "It is unlawful for any person to transact business in this state as a broker/dealer . . . unless he is registered under this act."

This means every person (legal entity) that falls within the definition of a broker/dealer must register with the Administrator of the state. Again, keep in mind that if a person falls under one of the exclusions from the definition, that person or legal entity does not have to register in the state.

T A K E N O T E

In addition, at the time of registration of a broker/dealer, any partner, officer, or director of the broker/dealer is automatically registered as an agent of the broker/dealer.

CASE STUDY   Who Is a Broker/Dealer?

Situation: First Securities Corporation of Illinois sells municipal bonds and equity securities to both the general public and other securities firms. First Securities sells many of its municipal bonds to its biggest customer, Transitions Broker/Dealers, Inc., located in Indiana. Transitions Broker/Dealers is a wholesale broker/dealer with no offices in Illinois that trades exclusively with other broker/dealers.

First Securities discovers that Transitions Broker/Dealers is not registered in Illinois but does business with other broker/dealers in Illinois. The president of First Securities asks the president of Transitions Broker/Dealers why his firm is not registered in Illinois; the president of Transitions answers that it is because they are not broker/dealers in Illinois. The president of First Securities is baffled—it appears to him that Transitions is indeed a broker/dealer.

Analysis: First Securities sells both exempt securities (municipal bonds) and nonexempt securities (equities) to the general public and to other broker/dealers. First Securities is a broker/dealer because it is a legal entity with a place of business in the state that effects securities transactions for itself and for the accounts of others and so must register in Illinois.

Like First Securities, Transitions Broker/Dealers conducts broker/dealer activities. However, in Illinois it confines the business to transactions between itself and other broker/dealers, such as First Securities. The USA specifically excludes from the definition of broker/dealer out-of-state broker/dealers who deal exclusively with other broker/dealers and have no place of business in the state.

Although Transitions Broker/Dealers is, in fact, conducting operations of a broker/dealer in Illinois, it does not meet the definition as stated in the USA and, therefore, is not subject to registration with the Illinois securities Administrator. If Transitions Broker/Dealers were located or had an office in Illinois, it would be a broker/dealer by definition and would have to register as such in Illinois.

What about the Indiana Administrator? Which of the firms must register? Even though Transitions Broker/Dealers only does a wholesale business, because it has an office in the state of Indiana, it would meet the definition of broker/dealer and would have to register as such. What about First Securities? Well, it depends on several factors we have not been told. Does First Securities maintain an office in Indiana? If it does, registration is required. If it does not and the only securities business it does is with other broker/dealers and financial institutions, it does not have to register in Indiana.

Financial Requirements

The Administrator may establish net capital requirements for broker/dealers. Think of net capital as the broker/dealer's liquid net worth. Net capital requirements of the states may not exceed those required by federal law, in this case, the Securities Exchange Act of 1934. The Administrator of a state may, however, require broker/dealers that have custody of, or discretionary authority over, clients' funds or securities to post surety bonds. The amount of surety bonds required by the states is limited to the amount set by the Securities Exchange Act of 1934. The Administrator may not require a bond of a broker/dealer whose net capital is in excess of that required by the SEC.

In lieu of a surety bond, the Administrator will accept deposits of cash or securities.

Effectiveness of Registration

Upon the applicant's submission of all required information to the state securities Administrator, the broker/dealer's registration becomes effective at noon on the 30th day after filing. The Administrator has authority to specify an earlier effective date as well as defer the effective date until noon of the 30th day after the filing of any amendment.

Registration Expiration

Broker/dealers' registrations expire on December 31 unless renewed.

QUICK QUIZ 1.2

True or False?

_T_ 1. In general, a person who effects transactions in securities for itself or for the account of others in the course of business must register in the state as a broker/dealer.

_T_ 2. Under the USA, an out-of-state firm that transacts business with an established customer who is on vacation is not considered a broker in the state in which the customer is on vacation.

_T_ 3. A person not defined under the USA as a broker/dealer in the state need not register as such.

AGENT

The USA defines an **agent** as any individual who represents a broker/dealer (legal entity) or an issuer (legal entity) in effecting (or attempting to effect) transactions in securities.

Agents are individuals in a sales capacity who represent broker/dealers or issuers of securities. As agents, they act, usually on a commission basis, on behalf of others who are known as principals. Other than on this exam, agents are usually referred to as registered representatives.

TAKE NOTE   The use of the term *individual* here is important. Only an individual, or a natural person, can be an agent. A corporation, such as a brokerage firm, is not a natural person—it is a legal entity. The brokerage firm is the legal person (legal entity) that the agent (natural person) represents in securities transactions.

Exclusions from Definition of Agent for Administrative Personnel

Clerical and administrative employees of a broker/dealer are generally not included in the definition of agent and, therefore, are not required to register. The logic for this exclusion from the definition should again be obvious. Clerical and administrative employees do not effect securities transactions with the public. They attend to the administration of the broker/dealer as a business organization. Under these circumstances, they are similar to employees of any other corporation.

The situation changes when administrative personnel take on securities-related functions. When they do so, they lose their exemption and must register as agents.

EXAMPLE

Secretaries and sales assistants (known as ministerial personnel) are not agents if their activities are confined to administrative activities, including responding to an existing client's request for a quote. However, if secretaries or sales assistants accept customer transactions or take orders over the phone, they are engaging in securities transactions and are subject to registration as agents.

Exclusions from the Definition of Agent for Personnel Representing Issuers

In many cases, individuals who represent issuers of securities are agents and therefore must register as such in the states in which they sell the issuers' securities. As discussed under the general topic of exemptions and exclusions, there are three exclusions from the definition of agent for individuals representing issuers. They are repeated here for emphasis. Individuals are excluded from the definition of agent and therefore are exempt from registration in a state when representing issuers in effecting transactions:

- in exempt securities;

- exempt from registration; and

- with existing employees, partners, or directors of the issuer if no commission or other remuneration is paid or given directly or indirectly for soliciting any person in this state.

Effecting Transactions in Exempt Securities

Securities exempt from registration are called **exempt securities**. An employee of an issuer is not an agent when representing an issuer in the following exempt securities:

- US government and municipal securities

- Securities of governments with which the United States has diplomatic relationships

- Securities of US commercial banks and savings institutions or trust companies (when not engaged in securities-related broker/dealer activities)

- Commercial paper rated in the top three categories by the major rating agencies with denominations of $50,000 or more and maturities of nine months or less

- Investment contracts issued in connection with an employee's stock purchase, savings, pensions, or profit-sharing plans

Once again, the exclusion from the definition of agent applies only when the individual does not receive compensation related to the amount or type of sales made.

QUICK QUIZ 1.3

Here are examples of questions you might see on the exam:

1. Under the Uniform Securities Act, the term *agent* would include an individual who represents an issuer in effecting transactions in
   A. a city of Montreal general obligation bond
   B. common stock offered by a commercial bank
   C. New Jersey Turnpike Revenue bond
   D. commercial paper with a maturity of 19 months

2. Under the Uniform Securities Act, the term *agent* would include
   A. an individual who represents an issuer in transactions in exempt securities
   B. an individual who represents a broker/dealer in a transaction in an exempt security
   C. a receptionist for a broker/dealer who directs calls for trade information to the appropriate individual
   D. the vice president of personnel for a national brokerage firm

---

Effecting Exempt Transactions

An employee of an issuer is not an agent when representing an issuer in the following exempt transactions. Transactions exempt from registration are called **exempt transactions.** They are:

- isolated nonissuer transactions;

- transactions between issuers and underwriters;

- transactions between savings institutions or trust companies; and

- private placements.

TAKE NOTE

An employee of an issuer is not an agent when representing an issuer if the issue is exempt from registration (e.g., banks, financial institutions, and governments). Additionally, the employee is not an agent when representing an issuer in exempt transactions (transactions between an underwriter and issuer). If the individual, however, receives compensation based on sales volume, registration as an agent is required. Exempt securities and exempt transactions will be covered in detail in the next Unit.

Agent Registration Requirements

The registration requirements for an agent that is not exempt are similar to those for a broker/dealer. The USA states, "It is unlawful for any person to transact business in this state as an agent unless he is registered under this act." In other words, an individual may not conduct securities transactions in a state unless that person is registered or exempt from registration in the state in which he conducts business. Furthermore, the act makes it unlawful for any broker/dealer or issuer to employ an agent unless the agent is registered.

An agent's registration is not effective during any period when the agent is not associated with a broker/dealer registered in the state. When an agent begins or terminates a connection with a broker/dealer or issuer, or begins or terminates activities that make him an agent, the agent and the broker/dealer or issuer must promptly notify the Administrator.

TAKE NOTE

When a broker/dealer registers in a state, the partners, officers, and directors are automatically registered as agents. In addition, when an agent shifts employment from one broker/dealer or issuer to another, all three persons—the agent, the old employer, and the new employer—must promptly notify the Administrator.

Financial Requirements

Unlike a broker/dealer, there are no financial requirements, or **net worth requirements**, to register as an agent. The Administrator may, however, require an agent to be bonded, particularly if the agent has discretion over a client's account.

CASE STUDY

Agent as Defined by the USA

Situation: The City of Chicago issues bonds for the maintenance of local recreational facilities. Purchasers have two choices: they can purchase the bonds directly from the city through Ms. Stith (an employee of the city responsible for selling the bonds), or they can purchase them from Mr. Thompson (an employee of First Securities Corporation of Chicago). Neither Ms. Stith nor Mr. Thompson charges a commission, although First Securities is remunerated with an underwriting fee.

Analysis: The City of Chicago is an issuer of exempt securities (municipal bonds). Ms. Stith, as an employee of the issuer (City of Chicago), is not an agent as defined in the USA because she is representing the issuer in the sale of an exempt security and receives no sales-based compensation. Therefore, Ms. Stith does not need to register as an agent with the Administrator of Illinois. However, Mr. Thompson, as a representative of First Securities, must register with the Administrator because he represents a broker/dealer in effecting securities transactions in the state. Representatives (agents of broker/dealers) must register in the states in which they sell securities.

TAKE NOTE   Exemptions from registration generally apply to individuals who represent issuers, rather than to individuals who represent broker/dealers.

If Ms. Stith received a bonus based on sales production, the USA would consider that as commission compensation and Ms. Stith would have to register as an agent.

Fee and Commission Sharing

Multiple Registrations

An individual may not act at any one time as an agent for more than one broker/dealer or for more than one issuer, unless the broker/dealers or issuers for whom the agent acts are affiliated by direct or indirect common control or the Administrator grants an exception.

Registered agents of broker/dealers may share fees or split commissions with others provided they are registered as agents for the same broker/dealer or for a broker/dealer under common ownership or control.

QUICK QUIZ 1.4   Write **A** if the person is an agent and **B** if not.

_A_   1. A person who effects transactions in municipal securities on behalf of a broker/dealer

_A_   2. An agent's salaried secretary who takes orders

_A_   3. An employee of a bank that is issuing shares who receives a commission for selling the bank's securities

_A_   4. An individual who represents her nonexempt employer in the sale of its securities to existing employees for a commission

_B_   5. A person who represents an issuer in effecting transactions with underwriters

---

INVESTMENT ADVISER

Under the USA, an **investment adviser** is defined as any person who, for compensation and as part of a regular business, engages in the business of advising others on the value of securities or on the advisability of investing in or selling them. The advice can be delivered in person, through publications or writings, or through research reports concerning securities.

Advice given on investments not defined as securities, such as rare coins, art, and real estate, is not investment advice covered by the USA or other securities legislation. As a result, persons providing such advice are not investment advisers. Again, definitions are crucial for determining whether an activity is subject to securities law.

To be an investment adviser under both state and federal securities law, a person must:

- provide advice about securities (not about jewelry, rare coins, or real estate);

- provide that advice as part of an ongoing business (hang a shingle and have an office for conducting business) on a regular basis; and

- receive compensation (payment for the advice).

TAKE NOTE   In most cases, investment advisers are legal persons, such as a partnership or corporation, that provide investment advice or portfolio management services on an ongoing basis. Investment adviser representatives work for investment advisers just as registered sales agents work for a broker/dealer. Note that a person can be an investment adviser if he operates as a sole proprietorship.

WHO ARE INVESTMENT ADVISERS?

An **investment adviser** is defined under both the Investment Advisers Act of 1940 and the USA as "any person who, for compensation, engages in the business of advising others as to the value of securities or the advisability of investing in securities or, as part of a regular business, issues analyses or reports concerning securities."

SEC RELEASE IA-1092

As a result of the proliferation of persons offering investment advice, Congress directed the SEC to define the activities that would subject a person to the Investment Advisers Act of 1940. The SEC did so in SEC Release IA-1092.

SEC Release IA-1092 interprets the definition of investment adviser under the Investment Advisers Act of 1940 to include financial planners, pension consultants, and others who offer investment advice as part of their financial practices.

Release IA-1092, in short, identifies as an investment adviser anyone who:

- provides investment advice, reports, or analyses with respect to securities;

- is in the business of providing advice or analyses; and

- receives compensation, directly or indirectly, for these services.

TAKE NOTE   If a person engages in these three activities, that person is an investment adviser subject to the Investment Advisers Act of 1940. As an investment adviser, this person must register with either the SEC or the states.

Provide Investment Advice

In Release IA-1092, the SEC maintains that a person who gives advice and issues reports, analyses, and recommendations about specific securities is an investment adviser if that person is in the business of doing so and receives compensation for the advice. This definition of investment adviser includes financial planners, pension consultants, and sports and entertainment representatives.

Financial Planners

Financial planners who make recommendations regarding a person's financial resources or perform analyses that concern securities are investment advisers if such services are performed as part of a business and for compensation. Under this interpretation, the SEC even includes financial planners who advise clients as to the desirability of investing in securities as an alternative to other investments, such as real estate, intangibles, or other assets.

Pension Consultants

Consultants who advise employee benefit plans on how to fund their plans with securities are also considered investment advisers by the SEC. In addition, under Release IA-1092, the SEC considers pension consultants who advise employee benefit plans on the selection, performance, and retention of investment managers to be investment advisers.

Sports and Entertainment Representatives

Persons who provide financially related services to entertainers and athletes that include advice related to investments, tax planning, budgeting, and money management are also investment advisers.

TAKE NOTE   A sports agent who secures a favorable contract for a football player and receives a commission of 10% of the player's salary is not necessarily an investment adviser. However, if the sports agent advises the football player to invest his money in specific securities, the agent is then in the business of offering investment advice and would then be subject to the Investment Advisers Act of 1940 or the Uniform Securities Act.

In the Business of Providing Advice

A person is in the business of providing advice and subject to regulation as an investment adviser if he:

■ gives advice on a regular basis such that it constitutes a business activity conducted with some regularity (although the frequency of the activity is a factor, it is not the only determinant in whether one is in the business of giving advice, and providing advice does not have to be the person's principal activity); and

■ advertises investment advisory services and presents himself to the public as an investment adviser or as one who provides investment advice.

TAKE NOTE

A person is in the business of giving investment advice if he receives separate compensation that represents a charge for giving the advice.

A person is in the business if he provides investment advice or issues reports on anything other than rare, isolated, and nonperiodic instances. In this context, a person is an investment adviser if he recommends that a client allocate funds to specific assets, such as high-yield bonds, technology stocks, or mutual funds.

A person whose business is to offer only nonspecific investment advice, through publication of a general newsletter, for example, is not covered by the act. However, such a person would be included if he acted as a representative of a broker/dealer and then made specific securities recommendations to clients.

Compensation

A person who receives an economic benefit as a result of providing investment advice is an investment adviser. Compensation includes advisory fees, commissions, and other types of fees related to the service rendered. A separate fee for the advice need not be charged; the fee can be paid by a third party on behalf of the beneficiary of the advice.

EXAMPLE

Fees that an investment adviser receives from a corporation for advice given to the corporation's employees or retirees are considered compensation. A financial planner who designs a comprehensive financial plan for the corporation's employees without charging a fee but receives commissions on insurance policies sold as part of the plan is acting as an investment adviser representative. Even though that compensation is indirect, it meets the release's definition of compensation for investment advice.

Exclusions from the Definition of Investment Adviser

As is the case with broker/dealers and agents, there are exclusions from the term *investment adviser*. Under the USA, the following are not investment advisers. They are excluded from the definition:

- Investment adviser representatives (the firm is the investment adviser, not the representative)

- Banks, savings institutions, and trust companies

- Lawyers, accountants, teachers, and engineers (LATE) whose investment advisory services are solely incidental to their professional practices

This exclusion is not available to any of the above professionals who have established a separate advisory business. Also, the exclusion would not apply to any of the above who holds himself out as offering investment advice.

The following also are excluded from the definition:

■ Broker/dealers whose investment advisory services are incidental to their brokerage business and who receive no special or separate compensation for offering advice

■ A publisher, employee, or columnist of a newspaper, news magazine, or business or financial publication; or an owner, operator, producer, or employee of a cable, radio, or television network, station, or production facility if, in either case, the financial or business news published or disseminated is made available to the general public and the content does not consist of rendering advice on the basis of the specific investment situation of each client

■ Federal covered investment advisers registered with the SEC (advisers with $30 million or more in assets under management or under contract to a registered investment company)

■ Any other person the Administrator specifies

Exemption from Registration for Investment Advisers

The USA exempts from registration certain persons who, although included in the definition of investment adviser, do not have to register as such in the state. These exemptions from registration are advisers who have no place of business in the state but are registered in another state, provided their only clients in the state are:

■ broker/dealers registered under the act;

■ investment advisers;

■ institutional investors, including large employee benefit plans;

■ existing clients who are not residents but are temporarily in the state;

■ limited to five or fewer clients, other than those listed above, resident in the state during the preceding 12 months (called the de minimis exemption); or

■ any others the Administrator exempts by rule or order.

TAKE NOTE   Because these exemptions all apply when the investment adviser does not have an office in the state, it is relevant to understand that an investment adviser or one of its representatives who advertises to the public, in any way, the availability of meeting with prospective clients in a hotel, seminar, or any other location in the state is considered to have an office in the state. However, an investment adviser representative who contacts clients in the state and notifies them that he will be passing through their town and is available to meet with them in his hotel room is not considered to have an office in the state because the announcement is being made only to existing clients and not to the public.

FEDERAL COVERED ADVISERS

The NSMIA made major changes in the way investment advisers register. The NSMIA divided registration responsibilities between the SEC and the states' securities departments. Basically, the largest firms are required to register with the SEC, and the smaller ones are required to register with the states.

Advisers registered with the SEC are known as **federal covered investment advisers.** Federal covered advisers are those:

- required to be registered or registered as an investment adviser with the SEC;

- excluded from the definition of an investment adviser by the Investment Advisers Act of 1940; or

- under contract to manage an investment company registered under the Investment Company Act of 1940, regardless of the amount of assets under management.

TAKE NOTE

Because so much of this exam deals with interpreting the laws, it is sometimes necessary to review some legal concepts. For example, if a person is excluded from the definition of investment adviser under the Investment Advisers Act of 1940, the states, under the NSMIA, cannot define such person as an investment adviser because federal law excluded that person from the definition. In other words, if the separate states could define the persons who were excluded from the federal definition as investment advisers, the federal law would have no meaning.

CASE STUDY

Out-of-State Advice

Situation: A California-registered investment adviser with no offices located in any other state has directed investment advice on five separate occasions over the past year to individual residents of the state of Nevada. Is the investment adviser required to register in the state of Nevada?

Analysis: The answer is no. Registration is not required because the investment adviser does not have an office in Nevada and directs business to five or fewer individual residents of the state during the year. If the firm had an office in Nevada, registration would be required in that state. Also, even if the firm had no office in Nevada, registration would be required if business had been transacted with six or more individual residents of the state during the previous 12 months.

If the business had been transacted with other investment advisers, broker/dealers, or institutional investors, there is no limit as long as there is no office in the state.

The NSMIA eliminated state registration for advisers with $30 million or more in assets under management. Advisers with at least $25 but less than $30 million have the option to register with either the state or the SEC. Advisers with less than $25 million must register with the state unless they do business in 30 or more states, in which case they must register with the SEC. The NSMIA stated that pension consultants with assets under control of at least $50 million would also be federal covered advisers.

Investment advisers exempt from state registration are not exempt from paying state filing fees and giving notice to the Administrator. The procedure is called **notice filing.**

CASE STUDY

Exclusions from Definition and Exemptions from Registration

Situation: Charles & Goode, a partnership located in Illinois, has been in the business of selling investment advice in the form of research reports and managing securities portfolios for the past 20 years. The partnership has earned a good reputation among investors and has managed less than $25 million until this year. This year, they gained several new clients and now have $50 million in assets under management.

Most of Charles & Goode's clients are wealthy individuals and residents of Illinois, but they have 3 clients who are residents of Wisconsin and 30 clients who live in Indiana. The principals of Charles & Goode have also formed a separate partnership called C&G Mutual Fund Advisers, Inc., which manages a small investment company with assets of $15 million. The partners of Charles & Goode are uncertain about what they must do to be in compliance with the registration requirements of the USA.

Analysis: As a partnership in the business of managing money for individual clients, Charles & Goode is included in the definition of investment adviser and must register as such with the Illinois securities Administrator until it manages $25 million or more in assets. However, with the addition of new clients as of the current year, Charles & Goode will be exempt from registration with Illinois, as it is now excluded from the definition of investment adviser. Charles & Goode is now a federal covered adviser that must register with the SEC because it has crossed the threshold of $30 million in assets under management.

Before becoming a federal covered adviser, Charles & Goode need not register in Wisconsin because they have five or fewer clients in the state; however, they must register in Indiana because they have more than five clients there. After becoming federal covered advisers, Charles & Goode does not have to register in Indiana, Wisconsin, or Illinois; after it manages more than $30 million, it only has to register with the SEC, not state Administrators. An adviser with assets of at least $25 million but not $30 million may register with either the state or the SEC. Advisers with $30 million or more in assets under management must register with the SEC only.

The separate partnership, C&G Mutual Fund Advisers, Inc., which manages only $15 million, is exempt from registration in Illinois (or any other state) because persons who operate as investment advisers to investment companies registered under the Investment Company Act of 1940, regardless of the size of the investment company, are federal covered advisers not subject to state registration. Both C&G Mutual Fund Advisers Inc., and the fund they manage may have to pay state filing fees under a procedure called **notice filing**.

TAKE NOTE

As a general rule, the SEC or federal rules involve bigger numbers than the state rules—large investment advisers must register with the SEC; small investment advisers must register with the state.

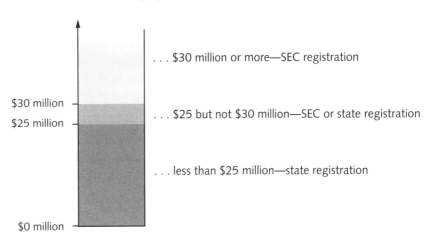

Adviser managing . . .

. . . $30 million or more—SEC registration

$30 million
$25 million

. . . $25 but not $30 million—SEC or state registration

. . . less than $25 million—state registration

$0 million

TEST TOPIC ALERT

An investment adviser registered under state law whose assets reach $30 million under management has 90 days to register with the SEC. A federal covered investment adviser whose assets under management fall below $25 million no longer qualifies for SEC registration and has 180 days to register with the state(s).

Financial Requirements

The Administrator may, by rule or order, establish minimal financial requirements for an investment adviser registered in the state. The Administrator may require an adviser who has custody of or discretionary authority over client funds or securities to post bonds or another form of security. The financial requirements that the Administrator sets cannot exceed those required by federal law. Usually, the bond is higher for custody than for discretion. Typically, the bond required of investment advisers with discretionary authority is $10,000, whereas advisers maintaining custody of customer funds and/or securities will need a bond or net worth of $35,000. In lieu of the surety bond, the Administrator will generally accept cash or marketable securities.

The USA specifies the action to be taken by a registered investment adviser whose net worth falls below the required minimum. By the close of business on the next business day, the adviser must notify the Administrator that the investment adviser's net worth is less than the minimum required. After sending that notice, the adviser must file a financial report with the Administrator by the close of business on the next business day.

QUICK QUIZ 1.5

1. Under the USA, the definition of investment adviser would include
   A. a bank
   B. a lawyer charging a fee to advise clients how to invest an injury settlement he just won for them
   C. an investment adviser representative
   D. none of the above

2. Under the USA, the term *investment adviser representative* would NOT include a(n)
   A. officer of a registered investment advisory firm whose responsibility includes supervision of solicitors
   B. associated person of the firm who, from time to time, makes specific recommendations to clients
   C. payroll clerk employed by an advisory firm whose responsibilities include computing the earnings of investment adviser representatives
   D. new employee of an advisory firm who has only been able to sign up 2 clients in his first 4 months

Registration Requirements for an Investment Adviser

The registration requirements for an investment adviser are much like those for a broker/dealer. The USA states, "It is unlawful for any person to transact business in this state as an investment adviser. . . unless he is so registered under this act or is exempt as described above from a state's registration requirements." In other words, persons included in the definition of investment adviser must register in the states in which they do business unless they are exempt from registration.

QUICK QUIZ 1.6

Write **A** if the phrase describes an investment adviser that must register under the USA and **B** if it does not.

_B_ 1. Publisher of a newspaper that renders general financial advice

_A_ 2. Broker/dealer that charges a fee for providing investment advice over and above commissions from securities transactions

_A_ 3. Investment adviser that manages $10 million in assets

WRAP FEE PROGRAMS

The exclusion offered to broker/dealers is lost when the brokerage firm earns special compensation for giving advice. One of the most common examples is the wrap fee program. In this type of asset management program, the broker/dealer wraps all of its services together, including transactions, advice, custody, and research, for one flat fee, usually a percentage of assets under management.

Because the wrap fee includes payment for securities advice, generally, the broker/dealer must be registered as an investment adviser and any agent participating must be registered as an investment adviser representative.

Firms offering these programs must make several critical disclosures to their clients, including:

- the amount of the wrap fee charged for the program;

- whether the fees are negotiable;

- the services provided under the program, including the types of portfolio management services;

- a description of the nature of any fees that the client may pay in addition to the wrap fee; and

- a statement that the program may cost the client more than purchasing these services separately (it is important that you remember this final disclosure for the exam).

INVESTMENT ADVISER REPRESENTATIVE

An **investment adviser representative** means any individual (other than an investment adviser or federal covered investment adviser) who represents an investment adviser or federal covered investment adviser when:

- making investment recommendations;

- managing accounts or client portfolios;

- soliciting investment advisory services; or

- supervising employees who perform any of these duties.

Investment Adviser: Business or Individual

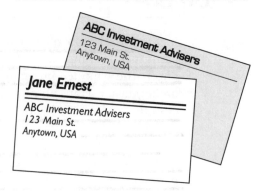

Investment Adviser Representative:
Individual Only

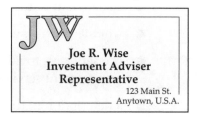

Exclusions from the Definition of Investment Adviser Representative

Registration of an investment adviser also leads to automatic investment adviser representative registration of partners, officers, or directors active in the business and anyone else performing a similar function. What does that really mean? An investment adviser representative can only be registered as a representative of a registered adviser, so individuals holding the positions mentioned above are in limbo until the adviser's registration becomes effective. At that time, their individual registrations go into effect. It does not mean that these people do not have to file applications and do not have to take the appropriate examinations.

Many independent financial planners operate as independent contractors, not employees of investment advisory firms or broker/dealers. Regardless, they are required to be registered as investment adviser representatives of the firm and must be placed under the same level of supervisory scrutiny as employees. Their business cards may contain the name of their separate planning entity but must also disclose the name of the entity registered as the investment adviser.

TEST TOPIC ALERT   Registered investment advisers are responsible for the supervision of individuals registered as investment adviser representatives, but acting in the capacity of independent contractors, to the same extent that they supervise those who are actual employees of the firm.

TAKE NOTE

Although not specifically tested, you should know that to become an investment adviser representative, one must pass either the NASAA Series 65 or Series 66 exam. In most jurisdictions, an NASD exam, such as the Series 6 or Series 7, must also be completed.

TEST TOPIC ALERT

Registration of a broker/dealer leads to automatic agent registration of partners, officers, or directors active in the business and anyone else performing a similar function. Registration of an investment adviser also leads to automatic investment adviser representative registration of the same category of persons.

QUICK QUIZ 1.7

True or False?

_F_ 1. An investment adviser representative must register with the SEC if she has clients with assets of $30 million or more under management.

_T_ 2. An investment adviser maintaining custody of a customer's securities or funds and exercising discretion in the account is generally required to maintain a minimum net worth of $35,000.

_F_ 3. An employee of an investment advisory firm is an investment adviser representative if his duties are limited to clerical activities.

_F_ 4. An administrative employee who receives specific compensation for offering investment advisory services is not an investment adviser representative.

_T_ 5. An employee of an investment advisory firm is an investment adviser representative if his duties involve making investment recommendations.

GENERAL REGISTRATION PROCEDURES

Any person who meets the definition of broker/dealer, agent, investment adviser, or investment adviser representative must register with the state. To register with the state securities Administrator, such persons must:

■ submit an application;

■ provide a consent to service of process;

■ pay filing fees;

■ post a bond (if required by the Administrator); and

■ take and pass an examination if required by the Administrator, which may be written, oral, or both.

SUBMITTING AN APPLICATION

All persons must complete and submit an initial application (as well as renewals) to the state securities Administrator. The application must contain whatever information the Administrator may require by rule and may include:

- form and place of business (broker/dealers and investment advisers);

- proposed method of doing business;

- qualifications and business history (broker/dealers and investment advisers must include the qualifications and history of partners, officers, directors, and other persons with controlling influence over the organization);

- injunctions and administrative orders;

- convictions of misdemeanors involving a security or any aspect of the securities business;

- felony convictions, whether securities related or not;

- financial condition and history;

- advertising and promotional material, if the applicant is an investment adviser; and

- Form ADV or similar document if the applicant is an investment adviser.

The Administrator also may require that an applicant publish an announcement of the registration in one or more newspapers in the state.

TAKE NOTE

If an agent terminates employment with a broker/dealer, both parties must notify the Administrator promptly.

If an agent terminates employment with Broker/Dealer I to join Broker/Dealer II, all three parties must notify the Administrator. If an investment adviser representative terminates employment with an investment adviser, notification requirements depend on how the investment adviser is registered.

If the investment adviser is a state-registered adviser, the firm must notify the Administrator. If the investment adviser is a federal covered adviser, the investment adviser representative must notify the Administrator.

PROVIDE CONSENT TO SERVICE OF PROCESS

New applicants for registration must provide the Administrator of every state in which they intend to register with a consent to service of process. The **consent to service of process** appoints the Administrator as the applicant's attorney to receive and process noncriminal securities-related complaints against the applicant. Under the consent to service of process, all complaints received by the Administrator have the same legal effect as if they had been served personally on the applicant.

The consent to service of process is submitted with the initial application and remains in force permanently. It does not need to be supplied with each renewal of a registration.

PAYMENT OF INITIAL AND RENEWAL FILING FEES

States require filing fees for initial applications as well as for renewal applications. If an application is withdrawn or denied, the Administrator is entitled to retain a portion of the fee. Filing fees for broker/dealers, investment advisers, and their representatives need not be identical. Broker/dealers or investment advisers may file, without a fee, an application for registration of a successor firm, whether or not the successor is then in existence, for the unexpired portion of the year.

The renewal date for all registrations is December 31. In the case of broker/dealers and investment advisers, a successor firm (an entity that acquires or takes over the operation of the existing firm) pays no fees until the renewal date.

POST-REGISTRATION REQUIREMENTS

The USA requires registered broker/dealers and investment advisers to keep accounts, correspondence, memoranda, papers, books, and other records the Administrator requires. These records must be preserved for three years by broker/dealers and five years by investment advisers unless the Administrator prescribes otherwise.

All records must be readily accessible (in the office) for the first two years.

The Administrator may also require registered broker/dealers and investment advisers to file financial reports. The recordkeeping and financial reports required by the state Administrator may not exceed those required by the Securities Exchange Act of 1934 or the Investment Advisers Act of 1940.

If any material information in these documents becomes inaccurate or incomplete, the registrant must promptly file a corrected copy with the Administrator. All required documents are subject to reasonable periodic, special, or other examination as the Administrator deems appropriate, in the public interest, or for the protection of the investor.

To avoid unnecessary duplication of examinations, the Administrator may cooperate with the securities Administrators of other states, the SEC, and any national securities exchange or national securities association registered under the Securities Exchange Act of 1934.

The Administrator's authority does not stop at the state line. The Administrator of any state in which the person is registered may demand an inspection during reasonable business hours with whatever frequency the Administrator deems necessary.

EFFECTIVENESS OF REGISTRATION

Unless a legal proceeding is instituted or the applicant is notified that the application is incomplete, the license of a broker/dealer, agent, investment adviser, or investment adviser representative becomes effective at noon 30 days after the later of the date an application for licensing is filed and is complete or the date an amendment to an application is filed and is complete. An application is complete when the applicant has furnished information responsive to each applicable item of the application. By order, the Administrator may authorize an earlier effective date of licensing.

In the same manner as a registration becomes effective on the 30th day after application, a request to withdraw registration also becomes effective on the 30th day after submission. However, should there be any legal proceedings in progress, the withdrawal will be held up until resolution of the issue. In any event, once withdrawal has taken place, the Administrator has jurisdiction of the former registrant for a period of one year.

QUICK QUIZ 1.8

1. Under the USA, which of the following automatically becomes registered as an agent when a broker/dealer registration becomes effective?
   A. Only the designated supervisory principal
   B. Any partner, officer, or person of similar status or similar function
   C. All agents currently registered with NASD through that broker/dealer
   D. No one

2. Under the USA, which of the following statements regarding the registration of a successor firm is(are) TRUE?
   A. The appropriate filing fee must be included with the application.
   B. The successor firm must be in existence before the filing of the application.
   C. The registration of the successor firm will be effective until the December 31 renewal date.
   D. All of the above.

QUICK QUIZ 1.9

True or False?

F 1. A consent to service of process must be submitted with each renewal application.

F 2. An Administrator may establish net capital requirements for investment adviser representatives.

F 3. When a securities professional registers in a state, he must provide the state Administrator with a list of all states in which he intends to register.

HOTSHEETS

For your convenience, Unit HotSheets summarizing the key points are located at the end of the manual on perforated pages.

UNIT TEST

1. Which of the following would be an agent under the terms of the USA?

   I.   A sales representative of a licensed broker/dealer who sells securities in the secondary markets to the general public
   II. An assistant to the president of a broker/dealer who, for administrative purposes, accepts orders on behalf of the senior partners
   III. A subsidiary of a major commercial bank registered as a broker/dealer that sells securities to the public
   IV. An issuer of nonexempt securities registered in the state and sold to the general public

   A. I and II
   B. I, II and III
   C. III and IV
   D. I, II, III and IV

2. A publicly traded corporation offers its employees an opportunity to purchase shares of the company's common stock directly from the issuer. A specific employee of the company is designated to process orders for that stock. Under the USA, the employee

   A. must register as an agent of the issuer
   B. need not register as an agent of the issuer under any circumstances
   C. may receive commissions without registration
   D. must register as an agent if he will receive commissions or remuneration either directly or indirectly

3. Registration as an investment adviser under the USA would be required for any firm in the business of giving advice on the purchase of

   A. convertible bonds
   B. gold coins
   C. rare convertible automobiles
   D. apartments undergoing a conversion to condominiums

4. Under the Uniform Securities Act, which of the following qualifies as an investment adviser representative?

   A. An employee, highly skilled in evaluating securities, who performs administrative or clerical functions for an investment adviser
   B. An individual who renders fee-based advice on precious metals
   C. A solicitor for an investment advisory firm who is paid a fee for his services
   D. An agent who offers incidental advice on securities as part of his sales commissions

5. Under the Uniform Securities Act, all of the following may provide investment advice incidental to their normal business without having to register as an investment adviser EXCEPT

   A. a teacher
   B. an economist
   C. a lawyer
   D. an engineer

6. Which of the following persons is defined as an agent by the Uniform Securities Act?

   A. Silent partner of a broker/dealer
   B. Secretary of a branch office sales manager
   C. Clerk at a broker/dealer who is authorized to take orders
   D. Broker/dealer executive who does not solicit or transact business

7. Under the Uniform Securities Act, any partner, officer, or director of a registered investment adviser is an investment adviser representative if he
   I. offers advice concerning securities
   II. manages client accounts or portfolios
   III. determines securities recommendations for representatives to disseminate
   IV. supervises personnel engaged in the above activities but does not sell these services to the public
   A. I only
   B. I and II
   C. I, II and III
   D. I, II, III and IV

8. Under the Uniform Securities Act, an agent is a(n)
   A. broker/dealer who sells registered securities to the general public
   B. individual who represents an investment adviser
   C. individual representing a broker/dealer who sells federal covered securities exempt from registration under the act
   D. individual who represents an issuer in an exempt transaction in which no commissions are paid

9. According to the Uniform Securities Act, which of the following is(are) considered a broker/dealer?
   I. An agent who issues securities for his own account and for clients of his employer
   II. An issuer of securities that are traded on SEC-registered exchanges
   III. A corporation that specializes in the sale of various oil and gas limited partnerships
   IV. A credit union that issues its own stock to depositors in proportion to the amount of the funds on deposit
   A. I only
   B. I and IV
   C. II and III
   D. III only

10. Under SEC Release IA-1092, an investment adviser is all of the following EXCEPT
    I. a broker/dealer who charges for investment advice
    II. a publisher of a financial newspaper
    III. a person who sells security analysis
    IV. a CPA who, as an incidental part of her practice, suggests tax-sheltered investments to her affluent clients
    A. I and II
    B. II and III
    C. II and IV
    D. III and IV

11. Under the Uniform Securities Act, the term *person* would include all of the following EXCEPT
    I. an unincorporated association
    II. a child prodigy, gifted in math, in the custody of his parents, for whom his parents opened an account at a major securities firm
    III. a political subdivision
    IV. an individual
    A. I, II and IV
    B. II only
    C. II and III
    D. III and IV

12. Under the USA, which of the following is considered a broker/dealer in a state?
    A. First Federal Company Trust
    B. XYZ broker/dealer with an office in the state whose only clients are insurance companies
    C. An agent effecting transactions for a broker/dealer
    D. A broker/dealer with no place of business in the state who only does business with other broker/dealers

13. Which of the following must register as an agent?
    A. An individual representing a broker/dealer who sells commercial paper
    B. An individual who sells commercial paper for ABC National Bank
    C. An employee of the Fed whose job is selling Treasury bonds to the public
    D. An individual who is paid a commission to sell certificates of deposit for ABC National Bank

14. An investment adviser hires 2 individuals to solicit new customers for the firm's wealth management service. Under the USA
    A. they may begin soliciting as soon as they have passed their licensing examinations
    B. soliciting is generally prohibited
    C. each of them would have to register as an investment adviser
    D. registration as investment adviser representatives is required

15. Which of the following would meet the definition of investment adviser under the Uniform Securities Act?
    I. A broker/dealer charging separately for investment advice
    II. The publisher of a weekly magazine, sold on newsstands, that contains at least 5 stock recommendations per issue
    III. A civil damages attorney who advertises that he is available to assist clients by suggesting appropriate investments for their successful claims
    IV. A finance teacher at a local community college who offers weekend seminars on comprehensive financial planning at a very reasonable price
    A. I only
    B. I, II and III
    C. I, III and IV
    D. I, II, III and IV

16. The term *investment adviser representative* would NOT include
    I. an employee of an investment adviser whose sole responsibility is filing paid bills and similar documents
    II. a receptionist operating the switchboard at the office of an investment adviser
    III. a minority stockholder whose only activity was soliciting new clients
    IV. the operator of the word processing equipment used as a desktop publishing system to prepare the adviser's weekly list of recommendations
    A. I and II
    B. I, II and III
    C. I, II and IV
    D. III only

17. All of the following statements regarding the powers of the Administrator are true EXCEPT
    A. the Administrator may request submission of literature used by the adviser to solicit new business
    B. the Administrator must be provided with a description of the adviser's proposed method of selecting investments
    C. an investment adviser's registration may be canceled if the firm is no longer in business
    D. the Administrator may rule that custody of client funds is not permissible

18. An investment adviser, having no place of business in the state, would be exempt from registration under the Uniform Securities Act if her only clients were
    I. banks or other financial institutions
    II. investment companies
    III. accredited investors
    A. I and II
    B. I and III
    C. II and III
    D. I, II and III

19. Which of the following statements regarding an investment adviser's withdrawal of registration under the Uniform Securities Act are TRUE?
    I. Unless a proceeding is involved, withdrawal will become effective 30 days after application unless the Administrator elects to shorten the period.
    II. Unless a proceeding is involved, withdrawal will be effective 30 days after application unless the Administrator elects to lengthen the period.
    III. Once withdrawal becomes effective, the Administrator can no longer commence an action against the former investment adviser.
    IV. If an action is commenced against the adviser after application for withdrawal is filed, but before the 30th day, effectiveness of the withdrawal is withheld until resolution of the action.
    A. I and III
    B. I and IV
    C. II and III
    D. II and IV

20. An investment adviser is exempt from registration under the Uniform Securities Act if he has no place of business in the state and his only clients are

    I. banks
    II. insurance companies
    III. residents of that state and none of his advice deals with securities traded on a national exchange
    IV. accredited investors

    A. I and II
    B. I, II and III
    C. I, II and IV
    D. I, II, III and IV

21. An investment adviser would be exempt from registration under the Uniform Securities Act if she had no place of business in the state and

    I. she offered her services to no more than 5 individuals in that state during any consecutive 12-month period
    II. she offered her services to fewer than 15 individuals in that state during any consecutive 12-month period
    III. her only clients were registered investment companies
    IV. her only clients were broker/dealers and other investment advisers

    A. I and III
    B. I, III and IV
    C. II and III
    D. II and IV

22. Under the Uniform Securities Act, if a broker/dealer were to become financially unsound, which of the following options might be used by the Administrator?

    I. Revoke the broker/dealer's license
    II. Suspend the broker/dealer's license
    III. Disallow renewal of the broker/dealer's license

    A. I and II
    B. I and III
    C. II and III
    D. I, II and III

23. A broker/dealer is registered in State X. It has no offices in State Y, although it does do business in that state. Under the Uniform Securities Act, registration in State Y is required if the client is a(n)

    A. bank
    B. broker/dealer
    C. insurance company
    D. investment adviser representative

24. Which of the following terms are synonymous?

    I. Salesman/Agent
    II. Dealer/Salesman
    III. Dealer/Agent

    A. I only
    B. I and II
    C. I and III
    D. II and III

25. Your primary source of earnings is the commissions generated on purchases and sales of securities by your customers. On occasion, you sell some of your clients mutual funds with 12b-1 fees, and, as a result, quarterly trails are paid to you even though no further money is being invested. Under the Uniform Securities Act

    A. you would be required to be registered as an investment adviser representative because your share of these asset-based fees would be considered special compensation
    B. you would be required to be registered as an investment adviser as your share of these asset-based fees would be considered special compensation
    C. this is permissible as long as you are currently licensed as an agent
    D. no further registration is necessary as long as the proper disclosures are made in the wrap fee disclosure document

ANSWERS AND RATIONALES

1. **A.** Under the USA, only individuals can be agents. A person who sells securities for a broker/dealer is an agent. An administrative person, such as the assistant to the president of a broker/dealer, is considered an agent if he takes securities orders from the public. Corporate entities are excluded from the definition of agent. Broker/dealers and issuers are not agents.

2. **D.** Under the USA, an individual is an agent when effecting transactions with an issuer's existing employees if commissions are paid. Therefore, there are cases where the employee would have to register as an agent.

3. **A.** Only persons in the business of giving advice on securities are required to register as investment advisers. Only the convertible bonds are securities.

4. **C.** A solicitor is considered an investment adviser representative under the Uniform Securities Act. An employee who performs only clerical or administrative functions is not an investment adviser representative. Precious metals are not securities; therefore, a person advising on them is not considered an investment adviser representative. An agent is a representative of a broker/dealer, and, as long as the only form of compensation is sales commissions, registration as an investment adviser representative is not required.

5. **B.** The Uniform Securities Act does not exclude economists from the definition of investment adviser as it does lawyers, accountants, teachers, and engineers who give advice that is incidental to the practice of their profession. Remember the acronym LATE—lawyers, accountants, teachers, and engineers. Test takers often mistake the E in LATE for economist.

6. **C.** Anyone who solicits or receives an order while representing a broker/dealer is an agent. Silent partners, administrative personnel, and executives of broker/dealers are not agents under the terms of the USA if they do not solicit or receive orders. Remember, broker/dealers are not agents; agents represent broker/dealers. If, however, any of these individuals were authorized to accept orders, registration as an agent would be required.

7. **D.** The Uniform Securities Act defines persons associated with an investment adviser as investment adviser representatives, including any partner, officer, or director who offers advice concerning securities. Persons who manage client accounts or portfolios, determine securities recommendations, or supervise personnel engaged in the above activities are investment adviser representatives.

8. **C.** An individual employed by a broker/dealer who sells securities to the public is an agent under the Uniform Securities Act. The USA defines an agent as "any individual other than a broker/dealer who represents a broker/dealer or issuer in effecting or attempting to effect purchases or sales of securities." The law excludes from the definition of agent individuals who represent an issuer in exempt transactions, exempt securities, and transactions with issuers' employees when no commission is paid. There is virtually no case in which a salesperson representing a broker/dealer is not an agent.

9. **D.** A corporation that sells securities to the public—in this case, oil and natural gas partnerships—is a broker/dealer as defined by the USA. Agents and securities issuers are not included in the definition of broker/dealer. Credit unions are not considered broker/dealers under the USA.

10. **C.** A publisher of a financial newspaper and a CPA who, as an incidental part of her practice, suggests tax-sheltered investments are not investment advisers. This answer would be the same under both the USA and federal law.

11. **B.** The term *person* is extremely broad. Excluded from the term would be a minor, a deceased individual, and one who has legally been determined incompetent.

12. **B.** Any broker/dealer with an office in the state, regardless of the nature of its clients, is defined as a broker/dealer under the USA. If the firm did not have an office in the state and its only clients were institutions (such as insurance companies) or other broker/dealers, it would be excluded from the definition. Banks or trust companies and agents are never broker/dealers.

13. **A.** An individual who represents a broker/dealer and sells commercial paper must register under the USA. The securities (commercial paper) are exempt; nevertheless, the representative must be registered as an agent of the broker/dealer. An individual who sells commercial paper for ABC National Bank would not have to register because the bank is excluded from the definition of broker/dealer and both the transaction and security are exempt from state registration requirements. An employee of the federal government need not register with the state because he represents an exempt issuer and is selling exempt securities without receiving compensation tied to sales. An individual who is paid a commission to sell certificates of deposit for a commercial bank does not have to register as an agent because he is not selling a security.

14. **D.** The definition of investment adviser representative includes individuals who solicit for the firm's advisory business.

15. **C.** Publishers of general circulation newspapers and magazines are excluded from the definition of investment adviser, even if the entire publication is devoted to investment advice. A broker/dealer loses its exclusion the moment it offers advice for a separate charge, as does an attorney who holds himself out as offering investment advice. Normally, a teacher is excluded, but not when charging for advice, as would appear to be the case here. On this examination, the term *comprehensive financial planning* always includes securities advice.

16. **C.** Clerical and administrative employees are not considered to be investment adviser representatives. Minority stockholder or not, someone involved in soliciting accounts would be an investment adviser representative.

17. **B.** It is not required that an investment adviser disclose to the Administrator the methods he uses to select investments.

18. **A.** Do not be mislead by the term *accredited investor*. It has absolutely no meaning other than when referring to a private placement of securities under the Securities Act of 1933. This term will appear frequently on the exam out of context (i.e., unrelated to private placements). Whenever it does, you can make the question easier by replacing the term with the phrase *ordinary public investor who needs all of the protection available under the law*. As long as the adviser has no place of business in the state, he is exempt from registration if his only clients are institutional investors such as banks, insurance companies, investment companies, other investment advisers, broker/dealers, $1 million or larger employee benefit plans, college endowment funds, and governmental units.

19. **B.** Withdrawal of registration normally becomes effective 30 days after application. The Administrator may shorten that period but may not lengthen it unless an action against the adviser is commenced. Once an action is commenced, withdrawal may not take effect until resolution of the case. The Administrator may take action against an adviser for up to 1 year after withdrawal.

20. **A.** An adviser with no place of business in the state is exempt if his clients are institutional (banks, insurance companies, investment companies, and so forth). There is no intrastate exemption, and the term *accredited investor* has no meaning here because it applies only to private placements under Regulation D of the Securities Act of 1933. This term will appear frequently on the exam out of context (i.e., unrelated to private placements). Whenever it does, you can make the question easier by replacing the term with the phrase *ordinary public investor who needs all of the protection available under the law.*

21. **B.** To enable an investment adviser to service a small number of clients in neighboring states without the hassles of registration, the de minimis requirements allow offers to up to 5 persons, other than institutional accounts, during any 12-month period. Fewer than 15 persons refers to the de minimis requirements of the Investment Advisers Act of 1940. There is no limit to the number of institutional clients (e.g., investment companies and broker/dealers) an out-of-state adviser can have and still be exempt from registration in that state.

22. **D.** The Uniform Securities Act is clear that insolvency is a cause for suspension, revocation, or denial of registration, whether we are talking about a broker/dealer or an investment adviser.

23. **D.** Broker/dealers must always register in a state if they do business with noninstitutional clients, regardless of the nature of the individual's employer.

24. **A.** *Agent* is another term for registered representative or salesman. An agent cannot be a broker/dealer; he can only work for one.

25. **C.** Even though we commonly associate fees with investment advice, the 12b-1 fee charged by some mutual funds is not considered to be the special compensation the law refers to when requiring registration as either an investment adviser or adviser representative. This is not a wrap fee program.

QUICK QUIZ ANSWERS

Quick Quiz 1.1

1. **F.** A corporation is a person under the law and is subject to the jurisdiction of the state Administrator with respect to securities transactions.

2. **F.** An individual is a natural person and, just like a legal person (e.g., a corporation), may be subject to the Uniform Securities Act.

Quick Quiz 1.2

1. **T.** A person who effects transactions in securities for itself or for the account of others must register in the state as a broker/dealer unless specifically excluded from the definition.

2. **T.** A firm with an out-of-state registration is not considered a broker/dealer in that state if transacting business with a customer who is passing through the state on vacation.

3. **T.** If a person is excluded from the definition, that person need not register as a broker/dealer; however, if he is not excluded, he must register.

Quick Quiz 1.3

1. **D.** As long as the individual represents the issuer in a transaction involving exempted securities, he is not included in the definition of agent. Notice that a 19-month commercial paper is not exempt, but the other choices are.

2. **B.** Most of the exclusions from the term *agent* refer to an individual representing an issuer. There is almost no case where an individual performing a sales function for a broker/dealer is not an agent. Clerical persons are not agents, nor are officers with no apparent sales function.

Quick Quiz 1.4

1. **A.** Persons must be registered as agents when they effect transactions on behalf of broker/dealers whether the securities are exempt or not.

2. **A.** Any individual taking orders on behalf of a broker/dealer must be registered whether or not they receive a commission.

3. **A.** An employee who represents an issuer of exempt securities (a bank) in selling its securities must register as an agent if he receives commissions. If no compensation were involved, registration would not be required because such an individual is not an agent.

4. **A.** A person who represents an employer in selling securities to employees must register as an agent if the person receives a commission. If no commission is paid, registration is not necessary.

5. **B.** Persons who represent issuers in securities transactions with underwriters need not register as agents as long as no compensation is paid. In the absence of a statement to the contrary, assume that there is no compensation.

Quick Quiz 1.5

1. **B.** Although lawyers are generally excluded from the definition of investment adviser, that exclusion holds true only if the advice given is solely incidental to the practice of the profession and no separate fees are charged. The separate billing here is what loses the exclusion. Remember, investment adviser representatives are not investment advisers, just as agents are not broker/dealers.

2.   **C.**   Clerical and administrative personnel are excluded from the definition of investment adviser representative. Remember, the definition includes anyone who makes recommendations (even if only upon occasion), manages accounts, solicits accounts, or supervises any of the above.

Quick Quiz 1.6

1.   **B.**   Publishers of newspapers and magazines of general circulation that offer general financial advice need not register.

2.   **A.**   Broker/dealers must register as investment advisers if they receive special or separate compensation for giving investment advice.

3.   **A.**   An investment adviser that manages less than $25 million in assets must register as an investment adviser under the USA. If the client is an investment company registered under the Investment Company Act of 1940, registration with the SEC is mandatory regardless of amount under management.

Quick Quiz 1.7

1.   **F.**   An investment adviser (not the investment adviser representative) must register with the SEC if the firm manages assets of $30 million or more. The individual would have to be registered as an investment adviser representative in the state in which her office is located.

2.   **T.**   An investment adviser maintaining custody of customer funds or securities must have a net worth of at least $35,000 regardless of whether or not the firm exercises discretion.

3.   **F.**   An employee of an investment advisory firm is not an investment adviser representative if his duties are confined to clerical activities.

4.   **F.**   Any employee who receives specific compensation for offering investment advisory services is considered an investment adviser representative.

5.   **T.**   Any employee of an investment advisory firm is an investment adviser representative if his duties involve making investment recommendations.

Quick Quiz 1.8

1.   **B.**   All individuals with management responsibility at the firm are automatically registered as agents when a broker/dealer becomes registered in a state, including officers, directors, and others performing similar duties.

2.   **C.**   No filing fee is necessary, nor is it required that the successor firm even be in existence at the time of filing. The registration is effective for the unexpired portion of the year and then must be renewed (with a renewal fee) each December 31.

Quick Quiz 1.9

1.   **F.**   A consent to service of process is filed with the initial application and permanently remains on file with the Administrator.

2.   **F.**   The term *net capital requirement* refers to the financial requirements of a broker/dealer, not an investment adviser representative. Investment adviser representatives may be required to post a bond if they maintain discretion.

3.   **F.**   A list of other states in which a securities professional intends to register is not required on a state application for registration.

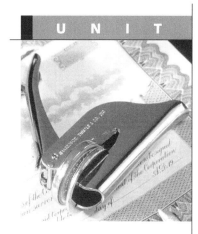

2

State Registration of Securities

State securities Administrators regulate securities transactions that occur in their states similarly to the way they regulate persons engaged in those transactions. This Unit discusses the procedures for the registration of securities as well as their exemptions from registration. For a securities transaction to be lawful under the USA, the security itself must be registered unless it or the transaction is exempt from registration requirements.

The Series 63 exam will include 15 questions on the material presented in this Unit. ∎

When you have completed this Unit, you should be able to:

- **recognize** what is and what is not a security;

- **determine** who is and is not a security issuer;

- **compare** and contrast the different methods of securities registration;

- **identify** instruments that are securities;

- **list** the categories of exempt securities;

- **define** an exempt transaction and provide examples; and

- **describe** the requirements for exemption from registration for private placements.

WHAT IS A SECURITY UNDER THE UNIFORM SECURITIES ACT?

Perhaps the most important term in the USA is the term *security*. Why is it so important? The reason is simple: the USA applies only to financial instruments that are securities. The purchase, sale, or issuance of anything that is not a security is not covered by the act. The definition of a security, however, is complex. Over the years, courts have determined case by case what constitutes a security. The US Supreme Court, in the Howey decision, defined the primary characteristics of what constitutes a security. For an instrument to be a security, the court held, it must constitute (1) an investment of money, (2) in a common enterprise, (3) with the expectation of profits, (4) to be derived primarily from the efforts of a person other than the investor. A common enterprise means an enterprise in which the fortunes of the investor are interwoven with those of either the person offering the investment, a third party, or other investors.

LIST OF SECURITIES UNDER THE UNIFORM SECURITIES ACT

The USA does not define the term *securities* but provides a comprehensive list of financial instruments that are securities under the act and therefore covered by its provisions. Under the USA, securities include:

- notes;
- stocks;
- treasury stocks;
- bonds;
- debentures;
- evidence of indebtedness;
- certificates of interest or participation in a profit-sharing agreement;
- collateral trust certificates;
- preorganization certificates or subscriptions;
- transferable shares;
- investment contracts;
- voting trust certificates;
- certificates of deposit for a security;
- fractional undivided interests in oil, gas, or other mineral rights;
- puts, calls, straddles, options, or privileges on a security;
- certificates of deposit or groups or indexes of securities;
- puts, calls, straddles, options, or privileges entered into on a national securities exchange relating to foreign currency;

- any interest or instrument commonly known as a security; or

- certificates of interest or participation in, receipts of, guarantees of, or warrants or rights to subscribe to or purchase, any of the above.

The following six items are not securities under the act:

Not securities {

- An insurance or endowment policy or annuity contract under which an insurance company promises to pay a fixed sum of money either in a lump sum or periodically

- Interest in a retirement plan, such as an IRA or Keogh plan

- Collectibles

- Commodities such as precious metals and grains

- Condominiums used as personal residences

- Currency

TEST TOPIC ALERT

The exam will want you to know what is and what is not a security. We suggest that you concentrate on learning the six that are not securities because they are much easier to remember and you will still be able to answer the questions correctly.

Examples of Nonsecurity Investments Versus Securities Investments

Although collectibles, precious metals, grains, real estate, and currencies can be attractive investments, they are not securities. Because these items are not securities, their sale is not regulated by state securities law. Furthermore, if a registered agent commits fraud in the sale of any of these items, he has not committed a violation of state securities law. He has violated the antifraud provisions of another act prohibiting fraudulent commercial transactions.

EXAMPLE

An individual farmer's direct ownership of a cow is not a security—it is just ownership of a cow. However, if the farmer makes an investment of money in a tradable interest in a herd of cattle on which he expects to earn a profit solely as the result of the breeder's efforts, he has purchased a security. In the same manner, if a condominium is purchased in a resort area with the goal of renting it out most of the year and it is used only for personal vacation time, the condo is considered a security because there is a profit motive, typically reliant on the efforts of a third party—the rental agent. On the other hand, if you have chosen to live in a condominium as a personal residence, it is a home, not a security.

TAKE NOTE

Annuities with fixed payouts are not securities, but variable annuities are because they are dependent on the investment performance of securities within the annuity.

NONEXEMPT SECURITY

A nonexempt security is a security subject to the registration provisions mandated by the USA. Exempt means not subject to registration. If a security is not registered or exempt from registration, it cannot be sold in a state unless in an exempt transaction. As you will see, the sale of an unregistered nonexempt security is a prohibited practice under the USA and may subject an agent to criminal penalties.

TAKE NOTE

The methods of registration discussed in this Unit refer to nonexempt securities. Think of what the legal terms actually mean in everyday usage. For example, a registered nonexempt security is most likely a common stock properly registered for sale in a state.

ISSUER

An **issuer** is any person who issues (distributes) or proposes to issue a security. The most common issuers of securities are companies or governments (federal, state, and municipal governments and their agencies and subdivisions).

If an issuer is nonexempt, it must register its securities in the states where they will be sold under one of the registration methods described in the Unit.

EXAMPLE

ABC Shoe Co. (a retail chain store) issues shares to the public. Mr. Bixby (an investor) buys the shares through his broker, Mr. Thompson, at First Securities Corporation. ABC Shoe is the issuer; Mr. Bixby is the investor; First Securities is the broker/dealer; and Mr. Thompson is the registered representative, known under the USA as an agent.

Issuer Transaction

An **issuer transaction** is one in which the proceeds of the sale go to the issuer. All newly issued securities are issuer transactions. In other words, when a company raises money by selling (issuing) securities to investors, the proceeds from the sale go to the company itself.

Nonissuer Transaction

A **nonissuer transaction** is one in which the proceeds of the sale do not go, directly or indirectly, to the entity that originally offered the securities to the public. The most common example is everyday trading on exchanges such as the New York Stock Exchange or Nasdaq. In a nonissuer transaction, the proceeds of the sale go to the investor who sold the shares.

If Mr. Bixby, an investor, sells 100 shares of stock he owns in ABC Shoe Co. (the securities issuer) on the New York Stock Exchange (NYSE), Mr. Bixby receives the proceeds from the sale, not ABC Shoes. This is a nonissuer transaction.

Nonissuer transactions are also referred to as **secondary transactions** or **transactions between investors**.

INITIAL OR PRIMARY OFFERING

An issuer transaction involving new securities is called a **primary offering**. If it is the first time an issuer distributes securities to the public, it is called an **initial public offering (IPO)**. Initial or primary offerings are issuer transactions because the issuer (the company) receives the proceeds from the investor investing in the company.

EXAMPLE   The first time that ABC Shoe Co. issued shares to the public, ABC Shoe engaged in an IPO, or a primary offering, because it received the proceeds from distributing its shares to the public. After ABC Shoe went public, transactions between its investors executed on exchanges through brokerage agents were secondary transactions in nonissuer securities.

QUICK QUIZ 2.1

1. Which list of instruments below is NOT composed of securities?
   A. Stock, treasury stock, rights, warrants, transferable shares
   B. Voting trust certificates, interests in oil and gas drilling programs
   C. Commodity futures contracts, fixed-payment life insurance contracts
   D. Commodity options contracts, interests in multilevel distributorship arrangements

2. The US Supreme Court defined an investment contract as having 4 components. Which of the following is NOT part of the 4-part test for an investment contract?
   A. An investment of money
   B. An expectation of profit
   C. Management activity by owner
   D. Solely from the efforts of others

3. Nonexempt securities
   A. need not be registered in the state in which they are sold
   B. always must be registered in the state in which they are sold
   C. need not be registered if sold in an exempt transaction
   D. need not be registered if sold in a nonexempt transaction

4.   A nonissuer transaction is a transaction
   A.   between 2 corporations in which one is issuing the stock and the other is purchasing
   B.   in which the issuing corporation will not receive the proceeds from the transaction
   C.   in which a mutual fund purchases a Treasury bond directly from the government
   D.   in which the security must be registered

Quick Quiz answers can be found at the end of the Unit.

REGISTRATION OF SECURITIES UNDER THE UNIFORM SECURITIES ACT

Under the USA, it is unlawful for any person to offer or sell a security in a state unless the security, transaction, or offer is exempt from the USA's registration requirements. If the security is not exempt or is not a federal covered security as defined by the NSMIA, it must be registered in the state or it cannot be lawfully sold in the state.

NATIONAL SECURITIES MARKETS IMPROVEMENT ACT OF 1996 (NSMIA)

The United States Congress, through its passage of the NSMIA, established the SEC as the regulator of nationally based securities activities, leaving the states with authority over state-based securities activities. Defining this relationship between state and federal regulation was accomplished under the NSMIA through the concept of federal covered securities.

A **federal covered security** is simply a security that has a federally imposed exemption from state regulation. Most securities sold today are federal covered securities.

CATEGORIES OF FEDERAL COVERED SECURITIES

The major categories of federal covered securities (securities covered by federal securities laws) that cannot be regulated by state securities Administrators include:

■   nationally traded securities, such as

   —   securities listed or authorized for listing on the NYSE and other SEC-registered exchanges, and

   —   securities included or qualified for inclusion in the Nasdaq National Market (but not those on the Nasdaq Capital Market);

- investment company securities registered under the Investment Company Act of 1940, such as

  — open-end management investment companies (mutual funds),

  — closed-end management investment companies,

  — unit investment trusts, and

  — face-amount certificates; and

- offers and sales of certain exempt securities, such as

  — securities offered to qualified purchasers under Regulation D of the Securities Act of 1933, and

  — securities offered by a municipal/governmental issuer, unless the issuer is located in the state in which the securities are being offered.

Nationally traded securities are securities that trade on the major exchanges regulated by the SEC. These exchanges register with the SEC and, in addition, are regulated by various self-regulatory organizations (SROs). The SEC, NASD, and the exchanges regulate nationally traded securities, so, as required by the NSMIA, states may not require registration. Such state regulation would be duplicative of federal registration.

Exempt securities (securities exempt from federal registration) are covered securities that states may not regulate. The most notable categories of exempt securities not subject to registration in the states are federal government securities, municipal securities, and private placements (Regulation D securities).

TAKE NOTE   Although investment company securities are federal covered securities, the USA allows states to impose filing fees on them under a process called notice filing, described below. Other federal covered securities are generally exempt from filing requirements.

Bonds issued by municipalities—for example, City of New York bonds due in 2020—are federal covered securities exempt from registration requirements in the states. However, there is an exception to the rule. States may require registration of municipal securities of their own states, but they may not require registration of municipal securities issued by other states. Why? Municipal securities of other states are covered securities exempt from state registration. Municipal securities issued in an Administrator's state are not covered securities; they are not covered by the exemption (states retain authority over the issue of the municipal securities by their own municipalities).

TAKE NOTE   Effective July 3, 2006, Nasdaq renamed the Nasdaq National Market as the Nasdaq Global Market. In addition, they created an even higher tier known as the Nasdaq Global Select Market. The Nasdaq Capital Market, formerly known as the SmallCap Market, remained unchanged. The effect of this change is that the top two tiers (i.e., anything with *Global* in it) are considered to be federal covered securities. There is no accurate way of determining when the exam will be updated to reflect this change, so please know both qualifications.

METHODS OF STATE REGISTRATION OF SECURITIES

The USA provides three methods for securities issuers to register their securities in a state. They are:

- notification or filing;
- coordination; and
- qualification.

NOTIFICATION (FILING)

The notification method of registering an issue—sometimes called registration by notification or registration by filing—applies to issuers who have registered their securities with the SEC under the Securities Act of 1933 but are not exempt from registration with the states in which they intend to distribute their shares. Such securities are nonlisted securities that trade interstate as opposed to within one state (intrastate), and as such, they must register by filing.

State registration under this method is accomplished by filing with the state copies of all records filed with the SEC (including amendments). Securities filed under this method, though registered with the SEC, are not federal covered securities.

TAKE NOTE   States can require the registration of the securities of public offerings by nonbank, nongovernment issuers whose securities are traded in marketplaces such as the Nasdaq Capital Market market or the OTC Bulletin Board. Notwithstanding the preemptive provisions of the NSMIA, state securities Administrators may require certain issuers whose securities are not traded on SEC-registered exchanges or the Nasdaq National Market to file copies of documents filed with the SEC for notice purposes.

Qualifications for Notification

To qualify for registration by filing, the issuer must have filed a registration statement with the SEC and:

- be organized under the laws of the United States or a state or have a designated American agent;

- have been in continuous operation for at least three years and have filed all required reports with the SEC during that time;

- have a class of equity securities of at least 400,000 shares held by at least 500 public shareholders—excluding securities held by officers and directors of the issuer, underwriters, and control persons owning 10% or more of that class of securities (warrants and options held by those persons cannot total more than 10% of the total number of shares);

- have either

— total net worth of $4 million, or

— total net worth of $2 million and net pretax income from operations for two of the last three years;

■ not have defaulted in the payment of principal, interest, or dividends in the current fiscal year;

■ for 30 days during the preceding three months, have at least four registered market makers; and

■ each underwriter of the security must be an NASD member who has agreed to a maximum commission of 10% of the offering price (offering price must be at least $5 per share).

Required Documentation for Notification

To register a security in a state by filing, consent to service of process and the following documentation are required:

■ A statement demonstrating eligibility for registration by filing

■ The name, address, and form of organization of the issuer; the amount of securities to be offered in the state; the states in which the offering will be registered; any adverse judgments pending; and a description of the security

■ If part of the offering is made on behalf of a nonissuer, the name and address of that nonissuer, the amount of securities held by that nonissuer, and the reasons for making the offering

■ A copy of the latest prospectus filed with the registration statement

If no stop order is in effect or no proceeding is pending, the documentation has been on file with the Administrator for five days, and the filing fee is paid before the effectiveness of the federal registration statement, the registration becomes effective concurrently with the federal registration.

If the federal registration statement becomes effective before conditions are met on the state level, the registration statement becomes effective when the conditions are satisfied.

Notice Filing for Federal Covered Investment Companies

There is one category of federal covered security that is always required to engage in a special form of state registration known as Notice Filing. Investment companies must file a notice with the Administrator and will be required to pay the specified fees. These fees are generally lower than for the other forms of state registration.

Under the notice filing procedure, state Administrators may require the issuer to file the following documents as a condition for sale of their securities in the state:

■ Documents filed along with their registration statements filed with the SEC

- Documents filed as amendments to the initial federal registration statement

- A report on the value of such securities offered in the state

- Consent to service of process

TEST TOPIC ALERT   Keep in mind the distinction between federal covered securities and SEC-registered securities. Under the NSMIA, federal covered securities are a narrowly defined group of securities that either trade on certain exchanges or are exempt from SEC registration. There are thousands of SEC-registered securities that do not meet the required standard, including those on the Nasdaq Capital Market.

Registration by Coordination

A security may be registered by coordination if a registration statement has been filed under the Securities Act of 1933 in connection with the same offering.

In coordinating a federal registration with state registration, issuers must supply the following records in addition to the consent to service of process:

- Copies of the latest form of prospectus filed under the Securities Act of 1933 if the Administrator requires

- Copy of articles of incorporation and bylaws, a copy of the underwriting agreement, or a specimen copy of the security

- If the Administration requests, copies of any other information filed by the issuer under the Securities Act of 1933

- Each amendment to the federal prospectus promptly after it is filed with the SEC

Effective Date

Registration by coordination becomes effective at the same time the federal registration becomes effective, provided:

- no stop orders have been issued by the Administrator and no proceedings are pending against the issuer;

- the registration has been on file for at least the minimum number of days specified by the Administrator, a number that currently ranges from 10 to 20 days, depending on the state; and

- a statement of the maximum and minimum proposed offering prices and maximum underwriting discounts and commissions have been on file for two full business days.

Registration by coordination is by far the most frequently used method.

Registration by Qualification

Any security can be registered by qualification. Registration by qualification requires a registrant to supply any information required by the state securities Administrator. Securities not eligible for registration by another method must be registered by qualification. In addition, securities that will be sold only in one state (intrastate) will be registered by qualification.

To register by qualification, an issuer must supply a consent to service of process and the following information:

- Name, address, and form of organization; description of property; and nature of business

- Information on directors and officers and every owner of 10% or more of the issuer's securities, and the remuneration paid to owners in the last 12 months

- Description of the issuer's capitalization and long-term debt

- Estimated proceeds and the use to which the proceeds will be put

- Type and amount of securities offered, offering price, and selling and underwriting costs

- Stock options to be created in connection with the offering

- Copy of any prospectus, pamphlet, circular, or sales literature to be used in the offering

- Specimen copy of the security along with opinion of counsel as to the legality of the security being offered

- Audited balance sheet current within four months of the offering with an income statement for three years before the balance sheet date

The Administrator may require additional information by rule or order. The Administrator may require that a prospectus be sent to purchasers before the sale and that newly established companies register their securities for the first time in a state by qualification.

Effective Date

Unlike coordination, in which the effective date is triggered by SEC acceptance of the registration, a registration by qualification becomes effective whenever the state Administrator so orders.

Regardless of the method used, every registration statement is effective for one year from its effective date. Unlike agent and broker/dealer registrations, the date December 31 is of no consequence. One interesting facet of the law is that the registration may remain in effect past the first anniversary if there are still some unsold shares remaining, as long as they are still being offered at the original public offering price by either the issuer or the underwriter.

QUICK QUIZ 2.2 True or False?

_T_ 1. ABC Shoe Company, a new retail shoe store chain, has applied for the registration of its securities with the SEC as required by the Securities Act of 1933 and wants to register its securities in the state of Illinois. ABC Shoe Company would most likely register by coordination.

_T_ 2. Any company may register by qualification whether or not it files a statement with the SEC.

EXEMPTIONS FROM REGISTRATION

In certain situations, the USA exempts both securities and transactions from registration and the filing of sales literature. A security, a transaction, or both can be exempt.

An exempt security retains its exemption when initially issued and in subsequent trading. However, an exempt transaction must be established before each transaction. The two are not mutually exclusive.

TAKE NOTE   A transaction can be exempt, but the security involved in that transaction may have to be registered.

The USA provides for a number of categories of exempt securities and even more categories of exempt transactions. Securities that are nonexempt must register. Certain federal covered securities do not register with the Administrator but file a notice with the Administrator. As mentioned above, an exempt security retains its exemption at its initial issue and in subsequent trading.

An exemption for a transaction, on the other hand, must be established with each transaction. Provided it is in the public interest, the state Administrator can deny, suspend, or revoke any securities transaction exemption other than that of a federal covered security.

TAKE NOTE   A security is exempt because of the nature of the issuer, not the purchaser.

An exempt transaction is exempt from the regulatory control of the state Administrator because of the manner in which a sale is made or because of the person to whom the sale is made. A transaction is an action and must be judged by the merits of each instance.

The USA prohibits the sale of securities in the state unless they are registered in the state, exempt from registration in the state, or subject to an exempt transaction. For example, an agent can sell a security that is not exempt in the state if the purchaser of the security is a bank or other institutional buyer. Because the sale is an exempt transaction, the sale can be made without registration. This means that the securities sold in exempt transactions do not have to be registered in the state. If such securities were not sold in exempt transactions, such as to an individual investor, they would have to be registered in the state.

TAKE NOTE

> The USA prohibits the sale of securities in the state unless they are registered in the state, exempt from registration in the state, or subject to an exempt transaction.

EXEMPT SECURITIES

Securities exempt from state registration are also exempt from state filing of sales literature. Exempt securities include the following.

- **US and Canadian government and municipal securities**. These include securities issued, insured, or guaranteed by the United States or Canada, by a state or province, or by their political subdivisions.

- **Foreign government securities**. These include securities issued, insured, or guaranteed by a foreign government with which the United States maintains diplomatic relations.

- **Depository institutions**. These include securities that are issued, guaranteed by, or a direct obligation of a depository institution (depository institution means any bank, savings institution, or trust company organized and supervised under the laws of the United States or any state). Securities issued by a savings and loan association are exempt only if the institution is authorized to do business in the state.

- **Insurance company securities**. These include securities issued, insured, or guaranteed by an insurance company authorized to do business in the state. Insurance company securities refer to the stocks or bonds issued by insurance companies, not the variable policies sold by the companies. Fixed insurance and annuity policies are not securities.

- **Public utility securities**. These include any security issued or guaranteed by a public utility or public utility holding company, or an equipment trust certificate issued by a railroad or other common carrier regulated in respect to rates by federal or state authority; or regulated in respect to issuance or guarantee of the security by a governmental authority of the United States, any state, Canada, or any Canadian province.

- **Federal covered securities**. These include any security of an issuer equal to or senior to the common stock, such as include rights, warrants, preferred stock, and any debt security.

- **Securities issued by nonprofit organizations**. These include securities issued by religious, educational, fraternal, charitable, social, athletic, reformatory, or trade associations.

- **Securities issued by cooperatives**. These include securities issued by a nonprofit membership cooperative to members of that cooperative.

- **Securities of employee benefit plans.** These include any investment contract issued by an employee stock purchase, saving, pension, or profit-sharing plan.

- **Certain money market instruments.** Commercial paper and banker's acceptances are the two most common examples.

TAKE NOTE

A promissory note (commercial paper), draft, bill of exchange, or banker's acceptance that matures within nine months, is issued in denominations of at least $50,000, and receives one of the three highest ratings by a nationally recognized rating agency is a federal covered security and also is exempt from registration requirements.

QUICK QUIZ 2.3

1. Which of the following securities is(are) exempt from registration and advertising filing requirements under the USA?
    I.   Shares of investment companies registered under the Investment Company Act of 1940
    II. Shares sold on the Nasdaq Global Market System
    III. AAA rated promissory notes of $100,000 that mature in 30 days
    IV. Shares sold on the New York Stock Exchange
    A. I only
    B. II, III and IV
    C. II and IV
    D. I, II, III and IV

2. Which of the following securities is NOT exempt from the registration and advertising requirements of the USA?
    A. Shares of Commonwealth Edison, a public utility holding company
    B. Securities issued by the Carnegie Endowment for Peace
    C. Securities issued by a bank that is a member of the Federal Reserve System
    D. Variable annuity contract issued by Prudential Insurance Co.

EXEMPT TRANSACTIONS

Before a security can be sold in a state, it must be registered unless exempt from registration or traded in an exempt transaction. This section covers exemptions for transactions that take place in a state.

There are many different types of exempt transactions. We begin by focusing on those most likely to be on your exam and finish with several others.

- **Isolated nonissuer transactions.** Isolated nonissuer transactions include secondary (nonissuer) transactions, whether effected through a broker or not, that occur infrequently (very few transactions per broker per year; the exact number varies by state). However, these usually do not involve securities professionals. In the same manner that individuals placing a "for sale by owner" sign on their front lawns do not need a real estate license, one individual selling stock to another in a one-on-one transaction is engaging in a transaction exempt from the oversight of the Administrator because the issuer is not receiving any of the proceeds and the parties involved are not trading as part of a regular practice.

■ **Unsolicited brokerage transactions**. These include transactions initiated by the client, not the agent. They are the most common of the exempt transactions. If a client calls a registered agent and requests that the agent buy or sell a security, the transaction is an unsolicited brokerage transaction exempt from state registration.

■ **Underwriter transactions**. These include transactions between issuer and underwriter as well as those between underwriters themselves.

■ **Bankruptcy, guardian, or conservator transactions**. Transactions by an executor, administrator, sheriff, or trustee in bankruptcy are exempt transactions.

■ **Institutional investor transactions**. These are primarily transactions with financial institutions.

■ **Limited offering transactions**. These include any offering, called a private placement, directed at not more than 10 persons other than institutional investors during the previous 12 consecutive months, provided that:

— the seller believes that all of the noninstitutional buyers are purchasing for investment purposes only;

— no commissions or other remuneration is paid for soliciting noninstitutional investors; and

— no general solicitation or advertising is used.

Unlike federal law, where the private placement rule restricts the number of purchasers, the USA restricts the number of offers that may be made.

■ **Preorganization certificates**. An offer or sale of a preorganization certificate or subscription is exempt if:

— no commission or other remuneration is paid or given directly or indirectly for soliciting any subscriber;

— the number of subscribers does not exceed 10; and

— no payment is made by any subscriber.

A preorganization certificate is a certificate to subscribe to an issue of securities. The certificate is issued before the organization of the issuer itself.

■ **Transactions with existing security holders**. A transaction made under an offer to existing security holders of the issuer (including persons who are holders of convertible securities, rights, or warrants) is exempt as long as no commission or other form of remuneration is paid directly or indirectly for soliciting that security holder.

- **Specified nonissuer transactions.** These include nonissuer transactions by a registered agent, provided that the security has been outstanding in the public's hands for at least 90 days and the issuer has:

  — registered a class of securities under the Securities Exchange Act of 1934; or

  — filed and maintained information comparable to that required under the Securities Exchange Act of 1934 with the Administrator for 180 days.

Most transactions that occur in federal covered securities, including securities of investment companies registered under the Investment Company Act of 1940, are traded in exempt transactions.

The following are examples of exempt transactions that are unlikely to be on your exam.

- **Nonissuer transactions by pledgees.** A nonissuer transaction executed by a bona fide pledgee (i.e., the one who received the security as collateral for a loan), as long as it was not for the purpose of evading the act, is a non-issuer transaction.

- **Unit secured transactions.** These include transactions in a bond backed by a real mortgage or deed of trust provided that the entire mortgage or deed of trust is sold as a unit.

- **Control transactions.** This includes mergers, consolidations, or reorganization transactions to which the issuer and the other person or its parent or subsidiary are parties.

- **Rescission offers.** These include offers made to rescind an improper transaction.

TEST TOPIC ALERT   Remember the distinction between an accredited investor and institutional investor. An **accredited investor** is an investor who meets the accredited investor standards of Regulation D. Regulation D standards require that an individual have a net worth greater than $1 million or $200,000 in income for the last two years and the current year, invest for his own account, and have requisite knowledge to evaluate investments. This term only applies to federal law, not the USA, and probably will never be the correct answer to a USA question.

An **institutional investor** is an investor that manages large amounts of money for other people, such as a mutual fund, an insurance company, a bank, or a pension fund.

Administrator's Powers

The USA grants the Administrator the authority, by rule or order, to exempt a security, transaction, or offer from registration and filing requirements. In addition, the Administrator may waive a requirement for an exemption of a transaction or security.

The Administrator may also revoke any exemption with respect to a security or transaction, other than that of a federal covered security, upon prior notice to the interested parties. The Administrator must also provide an opportunity for a hearing within 15 days of a written request. The Administrator also has the power to summarily deny or revoke exemptions pending final determination of any proceedings.

Under the USA, the burden of proving an exemption falls upon the person claiming it.

QUICK QUIZ 2.4

Indicate an exempt transaction with **Y** and a nonexempt transaction with **N**.

 1. Mr. Thompson, an agent with First Securities, Inc. (a broker/dealer), receives an unsolicited request to purchase a security for Mary Gordon, a high net worth individual

 2. The sale of an unregistered security in a private, nonpublicly advertised transaction offered to 10 or fewer investors over the last 12 months

 3. The sale of unclaimed securities by the Administrator of securities for the state of New Mexico

 4. Sale of stock of a privately owned company to the public in an initial public offering

5. Which of the following are exempt transactions?
    I.   An agent sells a security issued by a foreign government with which the United States has diplomatic relations to an individual client
    II. An unsolicited request from an existing client to purchase a nonexempt security
    III. The sale of an unregistered security in a private, nonpublicly advertised transaction to 14 noninstitutional investors over a period not exceeding 12 months
    IV. The sale of unlisted securities by a trustee in bankruptcy

    A. I and II
    B. I and III
    C. II and IV
    D. III and IV

STATE SECURITIES REGISTRATION PROCEDURES

The first step in the registration procedure is for the issuer or its representative to complete a registration application and file it with the state securities Administrator. The person registering the securities is known as the **registrant**.

FILING THE REGISTRATION STATEMENT

State Administrators require every issuer to supply the following information on their applications:

■ Amount of securities to be issued in the state

■ States in which the security is to be offered

■ Any adverse order or judgment concerning the offering by regulatory authorities, court, or the SEC

When filing the registration statement with the Administrator, an applicant may include documents that have been filed with the Administrator within the last five years, provided the information is current and accurate. The Administrator may, by rule or order, permit the omission of any information it considers unnecessary.

TEST TOPIC ALERT	Although most registration statements are filed by the issuer, the exam may require you to know that they may also be filed by any selling stockholder, such as a broker/dealer or an insider making a large block sale.

FILING FEE

The issuer (or any other person on whose behalf the offering is to be made) must pay a filing fee as determined by the Administrator when filing the registration. The filing fees are often based on a percentage of the total offering price.

If the registration is withdrawn or if the Administrator issues a stop order before the registration is effective, the Administrator may retain a portion of the fee and refund the remainder to the applicant.

ONGOING REPORTS

The Administrator may require the person who filed the registration statement to file reports to keep the information contained in the registration statement current and to inform the Administrator of the progress of the offering.

TAKE NOTE	These reports cannot be required more often than quarterly.

ESCROW

As a condition of registration, the Administrator may require that a security be placed in **escrow** if the security is issued:

■ within the past three years;

■ at a price substantially different than the offering price; or

■ to any person for a consideration other than cash.

SPECIAL SUBSCRIPTION FORM

The Administrator may also require, as a condition of registration, that the issue be sold only on a form specified by the Administrator and that a copy of the form or subscription contract be filed with the Administrator or preserved for up to three years.

TAKE NOTE

A registration statement may not be withdrawn by a registrant until one year after its effective date if any securities of the same class are outstanding and may only be withdrawn with the approval of the Administrator.

QUICK QUIZ 2.5

1. With regard to the registration requirements of the Uniform Securities Act, which of the following statements are TRUE?
   I. Only the issuer itself can file a registration statement with the Administrator.
   II. An application for registration must indicate the amount of securities to be issued in the state.
   III. The Administrator may require registrants to file quarterly reports.

   A. I and II
   B. I and III
   C. II and III
   D. I, II and III

PROSPECTUS DELIVERY REQUIREMENTS

As previously mentioned, the Administrator may require that, in the case of a security registered by qualification, the prospectus be delivered prior to the sale. For registrants using the other methods, the USA follows the rules of the Securities Act of 1933 requiring that delivery be no later than the mailing of the trade confirmation or actual delivery of the security.

HOTSHEETS

For your convenience, Unit HotSheets summarizing the key points are located at the end of the manual on perforated pages.

UNIT TEST

1. Which of the following is defined as a security under the Uniform Securities Act?
   A. A guaranteed, lump-sum payment to a beneficiary
   B. Fixed, guaranteed payments made for life or for a specified period
   C. Commodity futures contracts
   D. An investment contract

2. Under the Uniform Securities Act, which of the following persons is responsible for proving that a securities issue is exempt from registration?
   A. Underwriter
   B. Issuer
   C. State Administrator
   D. There is no need to prove eligibility for an exemption

3. Registration is effective when ordered by the Administrator in the case of registration by
   A. coordination
   B. integration
   C. notice filing
   D. qualification

4. The US Supreme Court in the Howey decision ruled that an instrument that represents the investment of money in a common enterprise with an expectation of profit solely through the managerial efforts of others is a security. According to the Howey decision, the USA would consider which of the following a security?
   A. Purchase of a house in a desirable real estate market with the expectation that the house will be resold at a profit within a few years
   B. Purchase of jewelry for speculative purposes as opposed to personal use
   C. Investment in options to acquire a security
   D. Investment in commodities futures

5. Under the Uniform Securities Act, which of the following would be considered an exempt transaction?
   I. An existing client calls to purchase 1,000 shares of a common stock that is not registered in this state
   II. The sale to an individual client of shares that are part of a registered secondary of a NYSE-listed company
   III. The sale of shares of a bank's IPO to an institutional client
   IV. The sale of shares of an insurance company's IPO to an individual client
   A. I and III
   B. I, III and IV
   C. II and IV
   D. I, II, III and IV

6. Which of the following securities is(are) exempt from the registration provisions of the USA?
   I. Issue of a savings and loan association authorized to do business in the state
   II. General obligation municipal bond
   III. Bond issued by a company that has common stock listed on the American Stock Exchange
   A. I only
   B. II only
   C. II and III
   D. I, II and III

7. A primary transaction is
   A. the first transaction between two parties in the over-the-counter market
   B. a sale between investors of securities traded on the New York Stock Exchange
   C. a new offering of an issuer sold to investors
   D. a secondary market transaction in a security recently offered to the public

8. All of the following describe exempt transactions EXCEPT

   A. ABC, a broker/dealer, purchases securities from XYZ Corporation
   B. First National Bank sells its entire publicly traded bond portfolio to Amalgamated National Bank
   C. Amalgamated National Bank sells its publicly traded bond portfolio to ABC Insurance Company
   D. Joe Smith, an employee of Amalgamated Bank, buys securities from ABC Brokerage Corporation

9. Under the USA, all of the following are exempt securities EXCEPT

   I. US government securities
   II. unsolicited transactions
   III. transactions between issuers and underwriters
   IV. securities of credit unions

   A. I, II and IV
   B. I and IV
   C. II and III
   D. IV only

10. Registration statements for securities under the Uniform Securities Act are effective for

   A. a period determined by the Administrator for each issue
   B. 1 year from the effective date
   C. 1 year from the date of issue
   D. 1 year from the previous January 1

11. Under the Uniform Securities Act, an issuer is any person who issues, or proposes to issue, a security for sale to the public. According to the USA, which of the following is(are) NOT an issuer?

   I. The City of Chicago, which is involved in a distribution of tax-exempt highway improvement bonds
   II. A partner in the AAA Oil and Gas Partnership, who sells his interest in the investment
   III. The AAA Manufacturing Company, which proposes to offer shares to the public but has not completed the offering
   IV. The US government, which proposes to offer Treasury bonds

   A. I only
   B. II only
   C. I, II and III
   D. I, II and IV

12. Which of the following transactions are exempt from registration under the USA?

   I. A trustee of a corporation in bankruptcy liquidates securities to satisfy debt holders
   II. An offer of a securities investment is directed to 10 individuals in the state during a 12-month consecutive period
   III. An agent frequently engages in nonissuer transactions in unregistered securities in his own account
   IV. Agents for an entrepreneur offer preorganization certificates to fewer than 10 investors in the state for a modest commission

   A. I and II
   B. I, III and IV
   C. I and IV
   D. II and IV

13. Which of the following is(are) primary transactions?

   I. John inherited securities of XYZ Corporation from his father who, as a founder of the company, received the shares directly from the company as a result of stock options.
   II. John sold the securities he had inherited from his father to his neighbor, Peter, at the market price without charging a commission.
   III. John's father, a founder of XYZ Corporation, purchased shares of XYZ directly from the corporation after its founding without paying a commission.
   IV. John purchased shares in XYZ Corporation in a third-market transaction.

   A. I only
   B. I and II
   C. III only
   D. I, II, III and IV

14. XYZ Corporation has been in business for over 20 years. It needs additional capital for expansion and determines that a public offering in its home state and neighboring states is appropriate. Which method of securities registration most likely would be used to register this initial public offering?

   A. Coordination
   B. Notice filing
   C. Qualification
   D. Any of the above

15. Which of the following meet the USA's definition of an exempt transaction?

   I. Transactions by an executor of an estate
   II. Transactions with an investment company registered under the Investment Company Act of 1940
   III. An unsolicited sale of a Bulletin Board stock
   IV. Sale of a new issue to an individual customer

   A. I and II
   B. I, II and III
   C. IV only
   D. I, II, III and IV

16. By order and with prompt notice, the Administrator could revoke the exemption of all of the following EXCEPT

   A. an Atlanta, Georgia, school district bond
   B. an unsolicited trade of a common stock listed on the American Stock Exchange
   C. a security issued by a fraternal organization
   D. a sale made to a bank

17. Which of the following are exempt securities?

   I. Securities guaranteed by domestic banks
   II. Securities issued by Canada
   III. Securities issued exclusively for religious purposes
   IV. Federal covered securities

   A. I, II and III
   B. II only
   C. II and IV
   D. I, II, III and IV

18. All of the following are exempt transactions EXCEPT

   A. transactions by a guardian
   B. sale of a registered IPO to an individual client
   C. unsolicited secondary market transactions
   D. transactions with a registered investment company

19. Most securities must be registered under state laws; however, certain securities are exempt under the act. One of the exemptions is the federal covered security, which covers

   I. any security listed on a major stock exchange
   II. all Nasdaq-listed securities
   III. securities meeting certain financial tests of liquidity and net worth
   IV. bank and insurance company securities

   A. I only
   B. I and II
   C. I, II and IV
   D. I and III

20. Under the Uniform Securities Act, the term *sale* would NOT include

   I. a dividend of 10 shares of stock for each 100 owned by shareholders of XYZ Corporation

  II. pledging $25,000 of listed stock to a bank as security for a loan made under normal banking practices

 III. MNT Corporation's acquisition of all of the stock of DEF Corporation in which it exchanged one of its shares for each two shares of DEF

A. I and II

B. I and III

C. II and III

D. I, II and III

ANSWERS AND RATIONALES

1. **D.** Investment contracts are defined as securities under the Uniform Securities Act. In fact, the term is often used as a synonym for a security. A guaranteed, lump-sum payment to a beneficiary is an endowment policy excluded from the definition of a security. Fixed, guaranteed payments made for life or for a specified period are fixed annuity contracts not defined as securities. Commodity futures contracts and the commodities themselves are not securities. Remember, it is much easier to remember what is not a security than what is.

2. **B.** The burden of proof for claiming eligibility for an exemption falls to the person claiming the exemption. In the event the registration statement was filed by someone other than the issuer (such as a selling stockholder or broker/dealer), that person must prove the claim.

3. **D.** Registration by qualification is the only registration method in which the Administrator sets the effective date. The effective date under registration by coordination is set by the SEC, and notice filing is merely the filing of certain documents enabling the registrant to offer securities in that state.

4. **C.** The investment in options is the only choice that meets the definition of security. It is an investment in a common enterprise with the expectation that the owner will profit as a result of the managerial efforts of others. The purchase of a house or jewelry is a purchase of a real asset or product that may result in a profit for the owner but not as a result of the managerial efforts of a third party. Commodities futures contracts are specifically excluded from the definition of a security. Note that options on futures, however, are securities under the USA. Remember the items that are not securities.

5. **A.** A client calling to purchase stock is an unsolicited transaction, probably the most common of the exempt transactions. Any sale to an institutional client is an exempt transaction while those to individuals, unless unsolicited, generally are not.

6. **D.** The USA exempts from registration a number of different issues, including securities issued by a bank or anything that resembles a bank (a savings and loan or a credit union). Securities issued by a governmental unit are always exempt. Securities listed on the American Stock Exchange are part of a group known as federal covered securities that also includes securities listed on the New York Stock Exchange and Nasdaq National Market issues.

7. **C.** A primary transaction is a new offering of securities by an issuer sold to investors. Transactions between two investors in the over-the-counter market are called secondary transactions (the market between investors). A sale between investors of securities traded on the New York Stock Exchange is another example of a secondary transaction.

8. **D.** The purchase of securities from a broker/dealer by an employee of a bank is a nonexempt transaction—it is a sale of a security by a broker/dealer to a member of the public and is therefore not exempt. Transactions between brokers and issuers, transactions between banks, and transactions between banks and insurance companies are exempt because they are transactions between financial institutions. Exempt transactions are most often identified by whom the transaction is with rather than by what type of security is involved.

9. **C.** Both unsolicited transactions and transactions between issuers and underwriters are exempt transactions, not exempt securities. US government securities and securities of credit unions are exempt securities, not exempt transactions.

10. **B.** Securities registration statements are effective for 1 year from the effective date.

11. **B.** Under the Uniform Securities Act, an issuer is any person who issues, or proposes to issue, a security. Examples of issuers are a municipality such as the city of Chicago, which issues tax-exempt highway improvement bonds; the AAA Manufacturing Company, which proposes to offer shares to the public even though it has not completed the offering; and the US government, when it proposes to offer Treasury bonds. Oil, gas, and mining partnerships are not issuers under the terms of the Uniform Securities Act; however, certificates of interest in them are securities. The resale of a partnership interest by an investor is a nonissuer sale because the investor is not the issuer.

12. **A.** Transactions by fiduciaries, such as a trustee in a bankruptcy reorganization, are exempt from registration. An offer of a securities investment to 10 or fewer individuals (called a private placement) is also exempt from registration. Engaging in nonissuer transactions on a regular basis is not exempt from registration. That exemption is granted only in the case of isolated transactions, the opposite of regular. Offers of preorganization certificates are not exempt when commissions are charged.

13. **C.** A primary transaction is one in which the issuer of the securities receives the proceeds of the sale. John's father, although a founder of the company, purchased shares directly from the company. This transaction is a primary transaction because the firm received the funds from the sale of the shares. In all the other instances, the firm, the original issuer of the securities, did not receive the proceeds of the transaction. These transactions are called nonissuer transactions.

14. **A.** Because this offering is being made in more than one state, SEC registration is necessary; the state registration method would be coordination, which is the simultaneous registration of a security with both the SEC and the states.

15. **B.** Transactions by a fiduciary, such as the executor of an estate, are included in the definition of exempt transaction, as well as transactions with certain institutional clients, such as investment companies and insurance companies. The OTC Bulletin Board is an electronic medium for the trading of highly speculative, thinly capitalized issues. Because the order is an unsolicited one, the transaction is exempt. Sale of a new issue of stock to an individual client would not be an exempt transaction.

16. **A.** Certain security exemptions may never be revoked by the Administrator. Most important among these exemptions are governments, municipals, insurance companies, and banks. The Administrator can revoke the exemption of a security issued by a specific nonprofit entity. The Administrator can also revoke the exemption of any exempt transaction. Remember the difference between an exempt security and an exempt transaction. Whether the security is exempt depends on who the issuer is. Whether the transaction is exempt depends on whom the trade is with or how the trade is made.

17. **D.** Among the exempt securities under the Uniform Securities Act (meaning exempt from the registration requirements) are securities issued by banks, securities issued by a recognized foreign government (particularly Canadian securities), securities issued by religious and other nonprofit organizations, and federal covered securities.

18. **B.** The sale of these registered securities to an individual would not be an exempt transaction.

19. **A.** The term *federal covered security* specifically applies to any security listed on a major stock exchange or the Nasdaq Global Market.

20. **D.** All 3 choices describe actions that are not deemed to be a sale under the Uniform Securities Act.

QUICK QUIZ ANSWERS

Quick Quiz 2.1

1. **C.** Commodity futures contracts and fixed payment life insurance contracts are included in our list of 6 items that are not securities. Commodity option contracts are securities.

2. **C.** Management activity on the part of the owner is not part of the Howey, or 4-part, test for an instrument to be a security. The 4 parts are: (1) an investment of money in (2) a common enterprise with (3) an expectation of profit (4) solely from the effort of others.

3. **C.** Nonexempt securities usually are required to be registered, but not always. If the nonexempt security is sold in an exempt transaction, registration may not be required.

4. **B.** A nonissuer transaction is one in which the company that is the issuer of the security does not receive the proceeds from the transaction. A nonissuer transaction is a transaction between two investors and may or may not require the security to be registered. Whenever the proceeds go to the issuer, it is an issuer transaction.

Quick Quiz 2.2

1. **T.** Registration by coordination involves coordinating a state registration with that of a federal registration.

2. **T.** Any company may register by qualification. Companies that are not established or that intend to offer their securities in 1 state register by qualification.

Quick Quiz 2.3

1. **D.** All of the securities are federal covered securities and therefore are not subject to the registration and advertising filing requirements of the USA.

2. **D.** Variable annuities (whose performance depends on the securities in a segregated fund) are nonexempt, which means they are covered by the act and have to be registered. Securities issued by regulated public utilities, charitable organizations, and banks that are members of the Federal Reserve System are exempt under the USA.

Quick Quiz 2.4

1. **Y.** Mr. Thompson's receipt of an unsolicited order from Ms. Gordon is an exempt transaction.

2. **Y.** The sale of an unregistered security in a private, nonpublicly advertised transaction to 10 or fewer offerees over the last 12 months is an exempt transaction (a private placement).

3. **Y.** The sale of unclaimed securities by the Administrator of securities for the state of New Mexico is an exempt transaction.

4. **N.** The sale of stock of a privately owned company to the public in an initial public offering is not an exempt transaction.

5. **C.** The private placement exemption is limited to 10-noninstitutional offerees, so 14 purchasers would certainly be over the limit. While a security issued by a foreign government with which we have diplomatic relations is an exempt security, a solicited sale by an agent to an individual client is not an exempt transaction.

Quick Quiz 2.5

1. **C.** The USA requires that any application for registration include the amount of securities to be sold in that state. The Administrator has the power to request regular filings of reports, but no more frequently than quarterly. Although the issuer is most commonly the registrant, selling stockholders and broker/dealers may also make application.

3

Unethical Business Practices

The USA was drafted for two primary reasons: (1) to eliminate conflicts in state securities legislation and make state securities laws uniform and (2) to protect the public from fraudulent securities practices. The protection against fraud, as well as unethical and prohibited practices, is the subject of this Unit. This Unit addresses what constitutes fraudulent practices under securities laws as well as what constitutes unethical and prohibited business practices as defined in the Statements of Policy issued by NASAA, the North American Securities Administrators Association.

Fraudulent, prohibited, and unethical practices are the most heavily tested topics. They make up 35% of the exam. You must know what these practices are and be able to apply the principles that guide ethical behavior to specific situations presented in the exam.

The Series 63 exam will include 21 questions on the material presented in this Unit. ■

When you have completed this Unit, you should be able to:

- **understand** the antifraud provisions of the USA;

- **recognize** specific fraudulent, unethical, and prohibited practices;

- **make** distinctions between prohibitions that pertain to the sale of securities and prohibitions that pertain to the sale of investment advice;

- **list** the required provisions for investment advisory contracts; and

- **identify** various types of deceptive market manipulation.

ANTIFRAUD PROVISIONS OF THE USA

Fraudulent activity may occur when conducting securities sales or when providing investment advice. Each of these categories is discussed separately. In general, **fraud** means the deliberate or willful attempt to deceive someone for profit or gain.

FRAUDULENT AND PROHIBITED PRACTICES IN THE SALE OF SECURITIES

The North American Securities Administrators Association (NASAA) has published a list of dishonest and unethical business practices for broker/dealers and their agents as well as one for investment advisers and their representatives. See Appendix A of this license exam manual for the policy relating to broker/dealers and agents and Appendix B for those giving investment advice. Appendix A and B are an integral part of this course and should be studied carefully.

State securities laws modeled on the USA address fraud by making it unlawful for any person, when engaged in the offer, sale, or purchase of any security, directly or indirectly, to:

■ employ any device, scheme, or artifice to defraud;

■ make any untrue statement of a material fact or omit to state a material fact necessary to make a statement not misleading; or

■ engage in any act, practice, or course of business that operates as a fraud or deceit on a person.

TAKE NOTE   There are no exceptions to the antifraud provisions of state securities laws. They pertain to any person or transaction whether the person or transaction is registered, exempt, or federal covered. Prevention of fraud is one of the few areas of securities law over which the states have full authority to act.

Although the USA does not list the prohibited practices, the following have been held by courts, regulatory agencies, and state Administrators to be fraudulent, dishonest, or unethical practices that will be prosecuted by state securities regulators.

The major categories of fraudulent and unethical behavior include:

■ misleading or untrue statements;

■ failure to state material facts;

■ using inside information;

■ making unsuitable investment recommendations;

■ exercising discretion without previous written authority;

- lending money or borrowing money or securities from clients;

- commingling customer funds and securities;

- guaranteeing client profits;

- sharing in client accounts; and

- market manipulation.

Misleading or Untrue Statements

Securities laws prohibit any person from making misleading or untrue statements of material fact in connection with the purchase or sale of a security. Not all facts are material. The law defines **material** as information used by a prospective purchaser to make an informed investment decision. In other words, when selling securities to their clients, agents must not deliberately conceal a material fact to encourage a client to buy or sell a security. Such act would constitute deceit for personal gain.

An agent inadvertently providing a client with an inaccurate address of a company whose shares the client was interested in purchasing would not be making an untrue statement of a material fact. Investors do not purchase shares on the basis of the company's street address. On the other hand, investors do make investment decisions on the basis of the qualifications of a company's management. Those qualifications would therefore be material fact. To misstate them is fraud.

The following are examples of material facts that constitute fraud if misstated by agents knowingly and willfully.

- **Inaccurate market quotations**—Telling a client a stock is up when the reverse is true is obviously an improper action. However, it would not be considered fraud if the inaccuracy resulted from a malfunction of the quote machine or an unintended clerical error. To be considered fraud, the action must be deliberate.

- **Misstatements of an issuer's earnings or projected earnings or dividends**—Telling a client that earnings are up, or that the dividend will be increased when such is not the case, is a fraudulent practice. However, it would not be fraud if you were quoting a news release that was incorrect.

- **Inaccurate statements regarding the amount of commissions, markup, or markdown**—There are circumstances where the amount of commission or markup may be higher than normal. That is permissible, as long as it is disclosed properly. However, telling a client that it costs him nothing to trade with your firm because you never charge a commission, and not informing him that all trades are done on a principal basis with a markup or markdown, is fraud.

- **Telling a customer that a security will be listed on an exchange without concrete information concerning its listing statue**—Years ago, before Nasdaq National Market (NNM) securities, an announcement that a stock was going to be listed on the NYSE invariably caused its market price to jump. Even though it does not have the same significance today (a better example would be a Nasdaq Capital Market stock going NNM), any statement of this type relating to a change in marketplace for the security is only permitted if, in fact, you have knowledge that such change is imminent.

■ **Informing a client that the registration of a security with the SEC or with the state securities Administrator means that the security has been approved by these regulators**—Registration never implies approval.

■ **Misrepresenting the status of customer accounts**—This behavior is fraudulent. Many people are not motivated to pay strict attention to their monthly account statements, making it relatively easy for an unscrupulous agent to fraudulently claim increasing values in the account when the opposite is true. Doing so would be a fraudulent action.

■ **Promising a customer services without any intent to perform them or without being properly qualified to perform them**—You say, "Yes, I can" to your client, even if you know you cannot deliver. For instance, the client asks you to analyze his bond portfolio to determine the average duration. Even though you do not know how to do that, you agree to do so. Under the USA, you committed fraud.

■ **Representing to customers that the Administrator approves of the broker/dealer's or agent's abilities**—This is another case of using the word *approve* improperly. A broker/dealer or agent is registered, not approved.

TEST TOPIC ALERT

Merely learning the terms is not enough to get you through the exam. On the exam, you must be able to identify situations in which the above violations occur. Be able to apply the concepts of fraud and unethical behavior to scenarios that are likely to occur in everyday business.

CASE STUDY

Making Leading or Untrue Statements

Situation: Mr. Thompson, a registered securities agent in Illinois, informs a long-standing client, Ms. Gordon, that her largest equity holding, First Tech Internet Services, Inc., will be listed on the NYSE upon completion of its application for listing. In addition, he exaggerates the earnings by $1 per share to make her more comfortable and encourage her to buy more shares. Mr. Thompson is convinced the earnings will rise to that amount and does not want Ms. Gordon to sell because he believes the stock will appreciate in price once listed on the Exchange. He also tells her that his firm will not be charging her any commission on the trade as they already have the stock in inventory, so she will be ahead from the start.

Analysis: Mr. Thompson violated the USA by deliberately misrepresenting the earnings of First Tech Internet Services. Although Mr. Thompson's motives may have been good, he must be truthful in his effort to encourage clients to purchase more stock—his conviction that the stock would rise upon its listing on the NYSE is not sufficient. No violation of the act occurred with respect to First Tech's Exchange listing because Mr. Thompson knew that the stock was in registration to be listed on the NYSE. To state that she will be ahead from the start because the firm will not charge a commission, but failing to state that a sale from inventory would include a markup, is a fraudulent act.

Failure to State Material Facts

The USA does not require an agent to provide all information about an investment, but only information that is material to making an informed investment decision. However, the agent must not fail to mention material information that could affect the price of the security. In addition, the agent may not state facts that in and of themselves are true but, as a result of deliberately omitting other facts, render the recommendation misleading under the circumstances.

CASE STUDY

Failure to State Material Facts

Situation: Upon NYSE acceptance of the listing application, there is an announcement that First Tech Internet Services will publish its financial statements in a newspaper advertisement. Mr. Thompson deliberately failed to mention this advertisement to Ms. Gordon.

After its listing on the NYSE, the research department in Mr. Thompson's firm prepares a negative report on First Tech. The research department discovered a change in accounting practices that will have a detrimental effect on subsequent earnings reported by First Tech. Mr. Thompson continues to recommend the stock to Ms. Gordon because he believes the increased exposure gained by the Exchange listing will outweigh the future decline in earnings. As a result, Mr. Thompson neglects to inform Ms. Gordon of the change before her purchase of additional shares.

Analysis: Mr. Thompson violated the USA even though he made no misleading statements to Ms. Gordon with respect to First Tech. Mr. Thompson did not have to mention the advertisement in the newspaper because it is not material, yet he violated the act when he failed to mention the accounting change that would result in significantly lower earnings. Although an accounting change is not ordinarily a material fact, in this case it was because it would have a detrimental impact on the company's earnings and its market price. An informed investor must have such information.

Using Inside Information

Making recommendations on the basis of material inside information about an issuer or its securities is prohibited. Should an agent come into possession of inside information, the agent must report the possession of the information to a supervisor or compliance officer.

TAKE NOTE

Material inside information under securities law is any information about a company that has not been communicated to the general public and that would likely affect the value of a security.

Using Inside Information

> **Situation:** Mr. Thompson is a friend and neighbor of Mr. Cage, president and owner of more than half of First Tech's securities. Mr. Cage discloses to Mr. Thompson that the company has just discovered a new technology that will double First Tech's earnings within the next year. No one outside of the company, except for Mr. Thompson, knows of this discovery. On this basis, Mr. Thompson buys additional shares of First Tech for Ms. Gordon.
>
> **Analysis:** The information on First Tech's new technology is material inside information that has not been made public. It is material information that only Mr. Thompson and company officials know. Mr. Thompson violated the USA by acting on this information. Mr. Thompson should have communicated the possession of the information to his compliance officer and refrained from making recommendations on the basis of this information.

Making Unsuitable Investment Recommendations

Agents must always have reasonable grounds for making recommendations to clients. Before making recommendations, the agent must inquire into the client's financial status, investment objectives, and ability to assume financial risk.

The following practices violate the suitability requirements under the USA as well as the rules of fair practice that regulatory agencies have developed. A securities professional may not:

- recommend securities transactions without regard to the customer's financial situation, needs, or investment objectives;

- induce transactions solely to generate commissions (**churning**), defined as transactions in customer accounts that are excessive in size or frequency in relation to the client's financial resources, objectives, or the character of the account;

- recommend a security without reasonable grounds; and

- fail to sufficiently describe the important facts and risks concerning a transaction or security.

Making Unsuitable Investment Recommendations

> **Situation:** Mr. Thompson has a wide variety of clients: high-net-worth individuals, trusts, retirees with limited incomes and resources, and college students. Mr. Thompson has strong beliefs about First Tech, a growth stock that pays no dividends. He forcefully recommends the stock to all his clients without informing them of the volatility of First Tech and the research department's pending downgrade in earnings. He also informs his clients of the new technology breakthrough that Mr. Cage, the president of First Tech, had told him in confidence.

Analysis: Mr. Thompson has violated the USA on several counts. First, he made a recommendation without regard to the separate financial conditions, needs, and objectives of his diverse client base. The recommendation is unsuitable for the investment objectives of his retired clients with fixed incomes and limited financial resources. In addition, he made the recommendation in an unsuitable manner by failing to reveal the earnings volatility or risk and the downgrade in earnings—and then he revealed inside information to clients while making recommendations on the basis of that information.

Exercising Discretion Without Prior Written Authority

Agents of broker/dealers may not exercise discretion in an account without prior written authority (power of attorney) from the client. Prior written authority is also known as trading authorization.

Discretion is given to an agent by the client when the client authorizes (in writing) the agent to act on his own and use his discretion in deciding the following for the client:

- Asset (security)

- Action (buy or sell)

- Amount (how many shares)

However, merely authorizing an agent to determine the best price or time to trade a security is not considered to be discretion.

CASE STUDY

Discretionary Trading Authorization

Situation: Mr. Thompson's client, Mr. Bixby, has indicated over the phone that he authorizes Mr. Thompson to make trades for him. Mr. Bixby's family lawyer, Mr. Derval, has specific power of attorney over some of Mr. Bixby's businesses. Mr. Bixby promised Mr. Thompson that he would send in the trading authorization within the next day or two to give Mr. Thompson discretion over the account. However, Mr. Thompson immediately executed trades in First Tech for Mr. Bixby to take advantage of its impending NYSE listing.

The following week, Mr. Thompson received Mr. Bixby's written discretionary trading authorization. On the day after the authorization arrived, Mr. Bixby's attorney, Mr. Derval, indicated that Mr. Bixby would like to buy shares in General Electric. Because Mr. Derval has power of attorney for Mr. Bixby, Mr. Thompson bought the shares.

Analysis: Mr. Thompson violated the USA by trading in Mr. Bixby's account before receipt of the written trading authorization. Having authorization in the mail is not sufficient. Mr. Thompson also violated the USA by accepting the order from Mr. Derval because although he is Mr. Bixby's attorney, he was not specifically authorized to trade in Mr. Bixby's securities account. The trading authorization signed by Mr. Bixby only gave authority to Mr. Thompson. Had Mr. Derval provided Mr. Thompson with specific written third-party trading authorization from Mr. Bixby, Mr. Thompson then could have accepted the order for General Electric without a violation of the act.

If Mr. Thompson is an investment adviser representative working for an investment adviser, he may exercise discretionary authority without obtaining written authority for 10 days after the date of the first transaction. (See Appendix B, point #2)

Loaning Money to or Borrowing Money or Securities from Clients

Securities professionals may not borrow money or securities from a client unless the client is a broker/dealer, an affiliate of the professional, or a financial institution engaged in the business of loaning money.

Securities professionals may not loan money to clients unless the firm is a broker/dealer or financial institution engaged in the business of loaning funds or the client is an affiliate.

Borrowing Money or Securities from Clients

Situation: On occasion, Mr. Thompson borrows cash from his discretionary client, Mr. Bixby, when Mr. Bixby's account is not fully invested. Mr. Bixby has given Mr. Thompson much latitude because Mr. Thompson has done well in managing the account and Mr. Thompson always repays the money in time to reinvest Mr. Bixby's funds in new securities purchases. Mr. Thompson justifies these borrowings as within the discretionary power Mr. Bixby had granted him. The First National Bank is also a client of Mr. Thompson, but he does not borrow from the bank because it charges unusually high interest rates.

Analysis: Mr. Thompson has engaged in a prohibited practice because securities professionals may not borrow from customers who are not in the business of lending money. Furthermore, Mr. Thompson violated the USA in exceeding the specific discretionary authority that Mr. Bixby had authorized. Mr. Bixby had authorized Mr. Thompson to trade in securities—not to take his money for personal use. Had Mr. Thompson decided to borrow from The First National Bank, it would have been permitted because it is an entity engaged in the business of lending money.

Commingling Customer Funds and Securities

Securities that are held in a customer's name must not be **commingled** (mixed) with securities of the firm.

If a firm has 100,000 shares of General Electric stock in its own proprietary account and its clients separately own an additional 100,000 shares, the firm may not place customer shares in the firm's proprietary account.

To mix shares together would give undue leverage or borrowing power to a firm and could jeopardize the security of client securities in the event of default.

One area of particular concern is brokerage firms maintaining margin accounts for their clients. In a margin account, the broker/dealer extends credit for the purchase of eligible securities and then uses those securities as collateral for the margin debt (loan). The pledging of these margin securities is known as

hypothecation. There are strict rules regarding how much of the client's securities may be hypothecated and requiring that the balance be segregated from the firm's own securities.

Guaranteeing Client Profits

Securities professionals may not guarantee a certain performance, nor may they guarantee against a loss by providing funds to the account.

TEST TOPIC ALERT

The term *guaranteed* under the USA means "guaranteed as to payment of principal, interest, or dividends." It is allowable to refer to a guaranteed security when an entity other than the issuer is making the guarantee. However, the regulatory agencies of the securities industry prohibit securities professionals from guaranteeing the performance returns of an investment or portfolio.

Sharing in Client Accounts

Agents cannot share in the profits or losses of client accounts unless the client and the broker/dealer supply prior written approval and the account is jointly owned. Furthermore, the gains and losses must be in proportion to the funds invested. In such a situation, it would be permissible to commingle the agent's and the customer's funds.

TAKE NOTE

An agent and a customer can have a joint account in which they share profits and losses in proportion to the amount invested. However, clients and a broker/dealer cannot have joint accounts.

TEST TOPIC ALERT

Unlike agents, investment adviser representatives are never permitted to share in the profits or losses in their client's accounts.

Market Manipulation

Securities legislation is designed to uphold the integrity of markets and transactions in securities. However, market integrity is violated when transactions misrepresent actual securities prices or market activity. The most common forms of market manipulation are front running and matching purchases.

Front running is the practice of entering an order for the benefit of a firm or a securities professional before entering customer orders.

EXAMPLE
If a securities professional receives an order from an institutional client to purchase a large number of shares, the securities representative or firm cannot enter a personal order before completing the customer's purchase in an effort to benefit from a likely price rise.

Matched purchases occur when market participants agree to buy and sell securities among themselves to create the appearance of activity or trading in a security. Increased volume in a security can induce unsuspecting investors to purchase the security, thereby bidding up the price. As the price rises, participants who initiated the matched purchases sell their securities at a profit.

TAKE NOTE
Arbitrage is the simultaneous buying and selling of the same security in different markets to take advantage of different prices; it is not a form of market manipulation. Simultaneously buying a security in one market and selling it in another forces prices to converge and, therefore, provides uniform prices for the general public.

OTHER PROHIBITED PRACTICES WHEN ENGAGED IN THE SALE OF SECURITIES

Security industry regulatory agencies have determined that the following practices may not violate any securities law but do violate industry standards of fair practice and, as a result, are prohibited:

- Deliberately failing to follow a customer's order

- Effecting transactions with customers not recorded on the books of the employing broker/dealer without express prior written consent, sometimes referred to as *selling away*

- Failing to bring written customer complaints to the attention of the employing broker/dealer

- Failing to inform customers that certain transactions involve larger than ordinary commissions, taxes, or transaction costs

- Soliciting orders for unregistered, nonexempt securities

- Spreading rumors

- Recommending transactions on the basis of rumors

- Failing to disclose capacity (did the firm act as a broker or a dealer?) on a trade confirmation

- Dividing or otherwise splitting the agent's commissions for the purchase or sale of securities with any person not also registered as an agent for the same broker/dealer or for an affiliated broker/dealer

- Backdating any records, including confirmations

■ Attempting to obtain a written agreement for a customer that he will not sue the agent even though the sale of certain securities is in violation of state law (any such agreement or waiver is not valid)

CASE STUDY

Practices—Trades Not on the Books

Situation: Mr. Thompson, a registered agent for First Securities, Inc., of Illinois, is also a part owner of Computer Resources, Inc., a privately held company in the state. Mr. Thompson is also a friend of Mr. Byers, the chairman of Aircraft Parts, Inc., a large manufacturing company traded on the NYSE. Mr. Byers has an account with Mr. Thompson at First Securities.

Mr. Thompson decides to sell his shares in Computer Resources to one of his clients. Because the shares are not publicly traded, Mr. Thompson completes the trades without informing First Securities or recording the transaction on their books. Mr. Thompson believes there is no need to inform his employer because the transaction was private. On the following day, Mr. Byers calls Mr. Thompson and indicates that he would like to sell his shares in Aircraft Parts. Mr. Thompson, who now has plenty of liquid assets from the sale of his shares in Computer Resources, decides to buy the shares directly from Mr. Byers. Mr. Thompson does not record the trade on the records of First Securities because he considers it a private transaction between himself and Mr. Byers.

Analysis: In both cases, Mr. Thompson has engaged in a prohibited practice. A registered agent may not conduct transactions with customers of his employing broker/dealer that are not recorded on the books without prior written consent. It makes no difference whether the shares Mr. Thompson sold were privately held; when an agent effects trades with clients of the firm, the transactions must be recorded on the books of the firm unless prior written authorization is obtained from the firm.

CASE STUDY

Practices—Customer Complaints and Front Running

Situation: Upon completion of the sale of his shares in Aircraft Parts, Inc., Mr. Byers has considerable funds to invest. Mr. Thompson then recommends to Mr. Byers that he purchase ABC Shoe Co., a thinly traded chain store that First Securities's analysts have highly recommended subsequent to its initial public offering. Mr. Byers agrees. Just before entering Mr. Byers's order, Mr. Thompson purchases several hundred shares for himself. Mr. Byers learned of Mr. Thompson's purchase and wrote him a stinging letter of complaint about it. Because Mr. Thompson considered the transaction a private matter, he did not think it necessary to bring the letter to the attention of First Securities. A few days later, Mr. Thompson personally apologized to Mr. Byers and took him out for a drink.

Analysis: Mr. Thompson has engaged in two practices that violate industry practice. First, although the recommendation of ABC Shoe Co. was perfectly appropriate, it was not appropriate for Mr. Thompson to enter his personal order for the same shares before completing Mr. Byers's purchase. This is known as front running, a prohibited practice. Additionally, Mr. Thompson (as a registered agent) must bring all written complaints to the attention of his employer. Had Mr. Byers simply lodged a verbal complaint, Mr. Thompson would not have been under an obligation to bring it to the attention of the manager of his office. Taking Mr. Byers out for a drink did not violate industry standards.

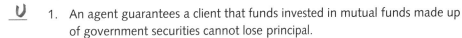

QUICK QUIZ 3.1

Write **U** for unlawful or prohibited activities and **L** for lawful activities.

_U_ 1. An agent guarantees a client that funds invested in mutual funds made up of government securities cannot lose principal.

_U_ 2. A nondiscretionary customer calls his agent and places a buy order for 1,000 shares of any hot Internet company. Later in the day, the representative enters an order for 1,000 shares of Global Internet Services.

_L_ 3. An agent receives a call from his client's spouse, advising him to sell her husband's securities. Her husband is out of the country and requested that his wife call the agent. The agent refuses because the wife does not have trading authorization, and she complains vigorously to his manager.

_U_ 4. A client writes a letter of complaint to his agent regarding securities that the agent had recommended. The agent calls the client to apologize and then disposes of the letter because the client seemed satisfied.

_L_ 5. A registered agent borrows $10,000 from a credit union that is one of her best customers.

_U_ 6. An agent is convinced that Internet Resources will rise significantly over the next 3 months. She offers to buy the stock back from her customers at 10% higher than its current price at any time during the next 3 months.

_L_ 7. An agent receives an order for the purchase of an obscure foreign security. The agent informs the client that the commissions and charges on this purchase will be much higher than those of domestic securities.

_U_ 8. An agent who works for a small broker/dealer that employs no securities analysts assures her clients that she can analyze any publicly traded security better than any analyst and that she will do it personally for each security purchased by a client, regardless of the industry.

_U_ 9. An agent recommends that her client buy 1,000 shares of Internet Consultants, Inc., an unregistered nonexempt security with a bright future.

Quick Quiz answers can be found at the end of the Unit.

FRAUDULENT AND PROHIBITED PRACTICES WHEN PROVIDING INVESTMENT ADVICE

The fraudulent and prohibited practices described in the previous section relate to the sale of securities. The USA also prohibits fraudulent and unethical activities by persons providing investment advice.

The USA makes it unlawful for any person who receives compensation (directly or indirectly) for advising another person (whether through analyses or reports) on the value of securities to use any device, scheme, or artifice to defraud the other person. Additionally, that person may not engage in any act, practice, or course of business that operates or would operate as fraud or deceit upon the other person or engage in dishonest or unethical practices as the Administrator may define by rule.

TAKE NOTE   Prohibitions are determined by the nature of the activity, not the registration status of the person engaged in the activity. Broker/dealers and their agents may give investment advice, yet not be included in the definition of investment adviser. Nevertheless, they are subject to the antifraud provisions of the act when they do provide advice. Why? The antifraud provisions of the USA refer to "any person" who commits fraud when selling securities or when providing investment advice with respect to securities.

FIDUCIARY RESPONSIBILITIES WHEN PROVIDING INVESTMENT ADVICE

When securities professionals act in an investment advisory capacity, they act as fiduciaries and are held to higher ethical standards than when they are engaged in the sales of securities. Fiduciary responsibility exceeds that which is normally required of ordinary business relationships because the fiduciary is in a position of trust. A fiduciary must act for the benefit of the client and place the interests of clients above their own. When securities professionals provide advice for a fee, they have a higher level of responsibility as fiduciaries.

Under the USA, an investment advisory contract must disclose:

- the services to be provided;

- the term of the contract;

- the amount of the advisory fee or the formula for computing the fee;

- the amount or manner of calculation of the amount of any prepaid fee to be returned in the event of contract termination;

- whether the contract grants discretionary power to the adviser or its representatives;

- that no assignment of the contract may be made by the adviser without the consent of the other party to the contract; and

- that, if the adviser is organized as a partnership, any change to a minority interest in the firm will be communicated to advisory clients within a reasonable period. A change to a majority of the partnership interests would be considered an assignment.

The act also prohibits certain performance fee arrangements contingent on capital gains or appreciation in the client's account. There is an exception, however, from the performance fee provisions for contracts with:

- a registered investment company;

- certain clients with more than $1 million in managed assets (usually institutions); or

- clients with $750,000 under the adviser's management or a net worth of at least $1.5 million (usually individuals).

A fee based on the average amount of money under management over a particular period is not considered to be a performance fee.

It is necessary for you to understand the technical definition of *assignment* as used in the acts. **Assignment** includes any direct or indirect transfer or pledge of an investment advisory contract by the adviser or of a controlling block of the adviser's outstanding voting securities by a stockholder of the adviser. If the investment adviser is a partnership, no assignment of an investment advisory contract is considered to result from the death or withdrawal of a minority of the partners or from the admission to the adviser of one or more partners who, after admission, will be only a minority interest in the business, whereas a change to a majority would be considered an assignment. However, a reorganization or similar activity that does not result in a change of actual control or management of an investment adviser is not an assignment

DISCLOSURE AND CONSENT

The act prohibits an investment adviser from effecting transactions as a principal with his clients or as an agent for his clients, unless his clients receive full written disclosure as to the capacity in which the adviser proposes to act and consent to do so before the completion (settlement) of the proposed transaction. This is unlike a broker/dealer who, when acting as a principal in a trade with a customer or as the customer's agent, need only indicate that capacity on the trade confirmation; consent is not required.

To provide some assurance that the act will not be violated, the regulators have recommended that each of the adviser's advisory clients be given in advance a written statement (brochure) prepared by the adviser that makes all appropriate disclosures. The disclosure statement should include the nature and extent of any adverse interest of the adviser, including the amount of compensation he would receive in connection with the account. This is particularly important if the adviser will be receiving compensation from sources other than the agreed-upon advisory fee. Furthermore, the adviser should obtain a written acknowledgment from each of his clients of their receipt of the disclosure statement.

The securities laws do not prohibit a registered investment adviser representative from being an employee of a registered broker/dealer. However, there would be a duty on the part of both the broker/dealer and the soliciting advisers to inform advisory clients of their ability to seek execution of transactions with broker/dealers other than those who have employed the advisers.

Disclosure must be made to all current clients and to prospective clients regarding material disciplinary action. The broadest definition of *material* would include any actions taken against the firm or management persons by a court or regulatory authority within the past 10 years. Required disclosure would include the following:

- State or regulatory proceedings in which the adviser or a management person was found to have violated rules or statutes that led to the denial, suspension, or revocation of the firm's or the individual management person's registration

■ Court proceedings, such as a permanent or temporary injunction, against the firm or management person pertaining to an investment-related activity or any felony

■ Self-regulatory organization proceedings in which the adviser or management person caused the business to lose its registration; the firm or individual was barred, suspended, or expelled; or a fine in excess of $2,500 or a limitation was placed on the adviser or management person's activities

During routine inspections, the regulators review an adviser's filings with the SEC or Administrator and other materials provided to clients to ensure that the adviser's disclosures are accurate and timely and do not omit material information. Examples of failures to disclose material information to clients would include the following.

■ An adviser fails to disclose all fees that a client would pay in connection with the advisory contract, including how fees are charged and whether fees are negotiable.

■ An adviser fails to disclose its affiliation with a broker/dealer or other securities professionals or issuers.

■ If an adviser has discretionary authority or custody over a client's funds or securities, or requires prepayment of advisory fees of more than $500 from a client six or more months in advance, the adviser fails to disclose a financial condition that is reasonably likely to impair the ability of the adviser to meet contractual commitments to those clients.

■ An adviser may defraud its clients when it fails to use the average price paid when allocating securities to accounts participating in bunched trades and fails to adequately disclose its allocation policy. This practice violates the act if securities that were purchased at the lowest price or sold at the highest price are allocated to favored clients without adequate disclosure.

QUICK QUIZ 3.2

1. The BJS Advisory Service maintains no custody of customer funds or securities, requires no substantial prepayments of fees, and does not have investment discretion over clients' accounts. Which of the following would have to be promptly disclosed to clients?
   I. The SEC has entered an order barring the executive vice president of the firm from association with any firm in the investment business.
   II. BJS has just been fined $3,500 by the NYSE.
   III. A civil suit has just been filed against BJS by one of its clients alleging that BJS made unsuitable recommendations.
   A. I and II
   B. I and III
   C. II and III
   D. None of the above

AGENCY CROSS TRANSACTIONS

Unlike broker/dealers, investment advisers are required to obtain the client's written consent, before the completion of the transaction, to act as principal or agent for that client. In an **agency cross transaction**, the adviser acts as agent for both its advisory client and the party on the other side of the trade. The act will permit an adviser to engage in these transactions provided the adviser obtains prior consent for these types of transactions from the client that discloses the following.

- The adviser will be receiving commissions from both sides of the trade.

- There is a potential conflict of interest because of the division of loyalties to both sides.

- On at least an annual basis, the adviser furnishes a statement or summary of the account identifying the total number of such transactions and the total amount of all remuneration from these transactions.

- The disclosure document conspicuously indicates that this arrangement may be terminated at any time.

- No transaction is effected in which the same investment adviser or an investment adviser and any person controlling, controlled by, or under common control with that investment adviser recommended the transaction to both any seller and any purchaser.

These requirements do not relieve advisers of their duties to obtain best execution and best price for any transaction.

***

EXAMPLE   An adviser has a client who is conservative and another who generally looks for more aggressive positions. The conservative client calls and expresses concerns about the volatility of First Tech Internet Services, Inc., stating that he thinks this may be the best time to exit his position. The adviser agrees and mentions that he has a risk-taking client who has expressed an interest in acquiring shares of First Tech and he would like to cross the security between the two clients, charging a small commission to each of them. With the permission of both parties, this transaction is not a violation.

***

TEST TOPIC ALERT   In an agency cross transaction, the adviser may not recommend the transaction to both parties of the trade.

Investment Advisory Contracts

The primary relationship between a client and an investment adviser is determined by an investment advisory contract. The USA makes it unlawful for an investment adviser to enter into, extend, or renew any investment advisory contract unless in writing, or the Administrator, by rule or order, provides otherwise.

CASE STUDY

Assignment and Notification of Change in Membership

Situation: Mr. Bixby withdrew $10 million from his account at the end of the year, leaving less than $750,000 under management with Market Tech Advisers, Inc., an advisory company incorporated in Illinois. During the course of the year, three officers left the firm. As a matter of corporate policy, Market Tech did not advise Mr. Bixby of these changes.

The following year, Market Tech (without notifying Mr. Bixby) assigned his account to Associated Investment Partners, a small partnership located in California, and Mr. Bixby was happy with the new partnership. Shortly after the assignment, Mr. Bixby learned of the death of one of the major partners through an article in the newspaper. He retained his account at Associated even though he had not been informed by them of the partner's death.

Analysis: Market Tech Advisers, Inc., was under no obligation to inform Mr. Bixby of the change in officers because it is a corporation and not a partnership. However, they did violate the USA by assigning Mr. Bixby's account to Associated Partners without his consent. Additionally, the USA requires partnerships to inform clients of any change in partner membership within a reasonable amount of time after the change, which means that Associated Partners violated the USA by not informing Mr. Bixby of the partner's death.

CASE STUDY

Investment Advisory Fees

Situation: Using the same client information as above, Market Tech Advisers, a registered investment advisory company, charges clients a fee of 1% of their assets managed by the firm on the basis of the average amount of funds in the account each quarter. In addition, for some of its high-net-worth clients, Market Tech charges a fee on the basis of the degree to which its performance exceeds that of the S&P 500. Last quarter, Market Tech's performance was extremely good and, as a result, the fees of one of its largest clients, Mr. Bixby, more than doubled. Next quarter, the value of the account dropped by 25% and so did the fee. Mr. Bixby complained that Market Tech was sharing in his capital appreciation in violation of the USA because he no longer had the required funds on deposit in the account.

Analysis: Market Tech is in compliance with the USA. Market Tech charged Mr. Bixby a 1% fee on the basis of the total assets in the account over a designated period as well as the stated performance fee. Because the assets increased and the performance beat the benchmark, so did the fee. Market Tech based its fees on the average value of funds under management and on a percentage of Mr. Bixby's capital gains—a practice in compliance with the USA for investors with a net worth at his level. Even though he no longer had $750,000 at the firm, his net worth was still in excess of $1.5 million. In the subsequent quarter, Market Tech's fee declined by 25% as a result of market deterioration. More than likely, no incentive fee was earned in this quarter.

TAKE NOTE
Any material legal action against the adviser must be disclosed to existing clients promptly. If the action occurred within the past 10 years, it must be disclosed to prospective clients not less than 48 hours before entering into the contract, or no later than the time of entering into such contract if the client has the right to terminate the contract without penalty within five business days.

Additionally, certain investment advisers are required to disclose any adverse financial condition that could impair the ability of the firm to perform its duties.

Brochure Rule

The USA requires investment advisers, when entering into an advisory contract, to deliver to prospective clients a written disclosure statement containing information containing their background and practices. This written disclosure statement must be delivered at least 48 hours before entering into the contract unless the advisory client has the right to terminate the contract without penalty within five business days after entering into the contract.

Thereafter, on an annual basis, the adviser must deliver, or offer to deliver, a copy of the brochure upon request.

The brochure rule permits the required disclosure to be made in one of two ways.

- The adviser may use Part II of Form ADV as the written disclosure statement.

- The adviser may use a written document containing the information required by Part II of Form ADV.

Custody of Client Funds and Securities

Under the USA, it is unlawful for an adviser to have custody of client funds and securities if:

- the Administrator in the state prohibits, by rule, advisers from having custody;

- in absence of a rule, an adviser fails to notify the Administrator that he has custody; and

- the adviser fails to supply clients, no less frequently than quarterly, with a statement of account activity and the location and amount of their assets.

Custody is the physical possession or control of funds and securities. Many advisers do not have custody because their client funds and securities are maintained at a bank or brokerage house. The adviser makes investment decisions under an advisory contract even though the client's funds and securities are placed in a custodial account at a commercial bank. Most Administrators will require advisers who maintain custody to provide a surety bond or meet certain net worth standards.

TAKE NOTE   The term *custody* does not include the use of discretion or advisory fees that represent prepayment.

TAKE NOTE   In April, 2004, the NASAA membership approved a change to the custody rules to basically parallel those incorporated earlier in that month in the Investment Advisers Act of 1940. We do not know when these rules will be tested on the exam, but here is a very short synopsis.

- Advisers may use qualified custodians to hold their customers funds and/or securities.

- Qualified custodians include banks and savings associations and broker/dealers.

- Clients must be promptly notified in writing of the qualified custodian's name and address and the manner in which the assets are being maintained.

- Account statements must be sent quarterly but may be sent by the qualified custodian instead of the investment adviser.

- If the quarterly statement is sent by the qualified custodian, the investment adviser has a fiduciary responsibility to make sure it was sent.

- A major benefit of having the qualified custodian do all of the work is that the investment adviser is relieved of the minimum net worth requirement of $35,000 and the obligation to furnish clients with an annual audited balance sheet. However, if the investment adviser exercises discretion, the $10,000 net worth requirement is still in effect.

OTHER PROHIBITED PRACTICES WHEN PROVIDING INVESTMENT ADVICE

- **Disclosing the identity or investments of a client without consent of the client, unless required by law.** An example of forced disclosure by law would be a subpoena to testify in a divorce case or a demand by the IRS to provide information about a client who is the subject of an audit.

- **Using third-party prepared materials without proper attribution.** Reports that are purely statistical in nature are excluded from this requirement, but a research report or market letter prepared by another entity could be used only if its authorship were disclosed.

- **Use of any advertisement** (defined as a communication to more than one person) **that uses any testimonial** (NASD rules do not prohibit testimonials, whereas the USA does). An advertisement may make reference to specific past performance of the adviser's recommendations as long as all recommendations of the same type of security for at least the past 12 months are included (not only the winners but the losers as well).

TEST TOPIC ALERT   Know how to recognize fraudulent, unethical, and prohibited practices. On your exam, you will be given various situations or scenarios and asked to determine which of NASAA's policy statements on ethical practices have been violated. NASAA's policy statements are contained in Appendix A and B. Review them carefully before you take your exam.

CURRENCY TRANSACTION REPORTS (CTRs)

The Bank Secrecy Act requires every financial institution to file a Currency Transaction Report (CTR) on FinCEN Form 104 for each cash transaction that exceeds $10,000. This requirement applies to cash transactions used to pay off loans, the electronic transfer of funds, or the purchase of certificates of deposit, stock, bonds, mutual funds, or other investments.

QUICK QUIZ 3.3

1. An investment advisory contract need not include
   A. the fees and their method of computation
   B. a statement prohibiting assignment of client accounts without client consent
   C. the states in which the adviser is licensed to conduct business
   D. notification requirement upon change in membership, if an investment partnership

True or False?

F   2. An Administrator may not prevent custody of securities or funds if an adviser notifies the Administrator before taking custody.

F   3. An adviser may not sell securities to its customers from its own proprietary account.

T   4. Under USA antifraud provisions, an investment adviser is bound by the restrictions that apply to sales practices when engaged in sales activities.

HOTSHEETS

For your convenience, Unit HotSheets summarizing the key points are located at the end of the manual on perforated pages.

U N I T   T E S T

1. Market manipulation is one of the prohibited practices under the Uniform Securities Act. Which of the following is an example of a broker/dealer engaging in market manipulation?

   I. Churning
   II. Arbitrage
   III. Front running
   IV. Matched trades

   A. I and II
   B. I, III and IV
   C. III and IV
   D. IV only

2. Your customer called to check on her account value at 9:00 am. You were unavailable at the time. It is now 2:00 pm, and you are able to call her back. Between 9:00 am and 2:00 pm, her account value dropped from $11,500 to $10,000. What should you say to her?

   A. "At the time you called, your account had a value of $11,500."
   B. "Your account value cannot be determined until the market closes."
   C. "Your account is valued at $10,000 at this time."
   D. "Your account was down to $9,700 earlier today but is now up to $10,000."

3. All of the following are prohibited practices under the USA EXCEPT

   I. borrowing money or securities from the account of a former banker with express written permission
   II. failing to identify a customer's financial objectives
   III. selling rights
   IV. supplying funds to a client's account only when or if it declines below a preagreed-upon level

   A. I and II
   B. I, II and III
   C. II and IV
   D. III only

4. A customer is upset with her agent for not servicing her account properly and sends him a complaint letter about his actions. Under the Uniform Securities Act, the agent should

   A. call the customer, apologize, and attempt to correct the problem
   B. tell the customer he is willing to make rescission
   C. do nothing
   D. bring the customer complaint to his employer immediately

5. Under the USA, the Administrator may deny or revoke a registration if an agent

   I. borrows money from his wealthy clients' accounts
   II. solicits orders for nonexempt unregistered securities
   III. buys and sells securities in accounts to generate a high level of commissions
   IV. alters market quotations to induce a client to invest in an attractive growth stock

   A. I, II and III
   B. I and III
   C. I and IV
   D. I, II, III and IV

6. Under the Uniform Securities Act, an investment adviser may legally have custody of money or securities belonging to a client if the

   I. adviser is not bonded
   II. Administrator has not prohibited custodial arrangements
   III. adviser does not also have discretionary authority over the account
   IV. adviser has notified the Administrator that he has custody

   A. I and III
   B. II only
   C. II and IV
   D. IV only

7. According to the USA, which of the following is an example of market manipulation?
   A. Creating the illusion of active trading
   B. Omitting material facts in a presentation
   C. Guaranteeing performance of a security
   D. Transacting in excess of a customer's financial capability

8. A federal covered investment adviser is one who
   I. has $30 million or more of assets under management
   II. manages an investment company registered under the Investment Company Act of 1940
   III. limits his advice to securities listed on the NYSE
   IV. is affiliated with a federally chartered bank
   A. I and II
   B. I and III
   C. II and III
   D. I, II, III and IV

9. Which of the following practices is prohibited under the USA?
   A. Participating in active trading of a security in which an unusually high trading volume has occurred
   B. Offering services that an agent cannot realistically perform because of his broker/dealer's limitations
   C. Altering the customer's order at the request of a customer, which subsequently results in a substantial loss
   D. Failing to inform the firm's principal of frequent oral customer complaints

10. An agent hears a rumor concerning a security and uses the rumor to convince a client to purchase the security. Under the USA, the agent may
    A. recommend the security if it is an appropriate investment
    B. recommend the investment if the rumor is based on material inside information
    C. recommend the security if the source of the rumor is reliable
    D. not recommend the security

11. If an agent thought that a technology stock was undervalued and actively solicited all customers, the agent
    I. did not violate the USA if all material facts were disclosed
    II. committed an unethical sales practice because the firm has not recommended this technology stock
    III. committed an unethical business practice
    IV. did not commit a violation if all clients were accurately informed of the price of the stock
    A. I, II and IV
    B. I and IV
    C. III only
    D. I, II, III and IV

12. Which of the following transactions are prohibited?
    I. Borrowing money or securities from a high net worth customer
    II. Selling speculative or hot issues to a retired couple of modest means on a fixed income
    III. Failing to follow a customer's orders so as to prevent investment in a security not adequately covered by well-known securities analysts
    IV. Backdating confirmations for the benefit of the client's tax reporting
    A. I and II
    B. I, II and III
    C. II and III
    D. I, II, III and IV

13. It is legal under the USA for a registered investment adviser to tell a client that

   A. a registered security may lawfully be sold in that state
   B. an exempt security is not required to be registered because it is generally regarded as being safer than a nonexempt security
   C. the adviser's qualifications have been found satisfactory by the Administrator
   D. a registered security has been approved for sale in the state by the Administrator

14. An agent omits facts that a prudent investor requires to make informed decisions. Under the Uniform Securities Act, this action is

   A. fraudulent for nonexempt securities only
   B. fraudulent for exempt securities only
   C. fraudulent for both exempt and nonexempt securities
   D. not fraudulent if there was willful intent to omit the information

15. Which of the following actions is NOT a prohibited practice under the USA?

   A. A market maker fills his firm's order ahead of a customer order at the same price.
   B. A specialist on the NYSE buys and sells stock as principal.
   C. A principal of a broker/dealer allows a rumor to spread that ABC is going to acquire LMN; after a few days, the broker/dealer sells ABC short for its own account.
   D. An agent sells a customer's stock at the bid price and makes up the difference with a personal check.

16. Which of the following is(are) prohibited under the USA?

   I. Recommending tax shelters to low-income retirees
   II. Stating that a state Administrator has approved an offering on the basis of the quality of information found in the prospectus
   III. Soliciting orders for unregistered, nonexempt securities
   IV. Employing any device to defraud

   A. I only
   B. I and II
   C. I, II and III
   D. I, II, III and IV

17. According to the Uniform Securities Act, an investment adviser may have custody of a customer's funds and securities if

   A. it has received the permission of the Administrator
   B. it has received permission from the SEC
   C. it does not share in the capital gains of the account
   D. the Administrator has been informed of the custody

18. According to the USA, which of the following is a prohibited activity?

   A. The agent enters into an agreement to share in the profits/losses of the customer's account without an investment in the account.
   B. The agent and his spouse jointly own their own personal trading account at the firm.
   C. The agent, with his firm's and the client's permission, participates in the profits and losses of the customer's account in proportion to his investment in the account.
   D. An agent refuses a client's request to share in the performance of the client's account.

19. A registered broker/dealer is under common control with a registered investment adviser. An individual who is an agent of the broker/dealer and an investment adviser representative of the adviser has a client with $250,000 under an asset management program. This individual calls the client and suggests the purchase of 500 shares of RMBM common stock as an appropriate addition to the portfolio. The broker/dealer is a market maker in RMBM, and the sale will be made as a principal, a fact that is disclosed to the client on the trade confirmation. In this situation, the registered person has acted

   A. lawfully in that the disclosure of capacity was made on the confirmation
   B. lawfully in that disclosure of capacity is not necessary when executing trades in managed accounts
   C. unlawfully in that any stock in which the broker/dealer is a market maker is probably not suitable for a managed money client
   D. unlawfully in that investment advisers are required to make written disclosure before completion of a trade in which the firm or an affiliate will be acting in a principal capacity and receive the client's consent

20. Which of the following are prohibited practices?
   I. An investment advisory firm organized as a partnership failed to inform its clients of the departure of a partner with a very small interest in the partnership.
   II. An investment advisory firm charges an annual fee equal to 2% of the first $250,000 in assets under management, 1% of the next $500,000, and .5% for everything in excess of $750,000.
   III. The majority stockholder of a registered investment adviser pledges his stock as collateral for a loan taken out by the firm to expand its services without obtaining client consent for assignment of their contracts.
   IV. An adviser engages in agency cross transactions.

   A. I and III
   B. I and IV
   C. III and IV
   D. I, II, III and IV

21. ZAP Brokerage has 5 partners. Raymond Zap, Jr., is a minor partner. He violates the USA because he did not perform his job of making sure that the firm maintained the minimum required capital. Which of the following are TRUE?
   I. Only Raymond will have his license suspended.
   II. The Administrator may revoke the entire firm's right to sell securities.
   III. A revocation of ZAP's registration would cause each of its agent's registrations to be terminated.
   IV. The firm could be fined up to $5,000 but incur no suspension.

   A. I and II
   B. II and III
   C. III and IV
   D. I, II, III and IV

22. When may the intentional omission of a fact in a securities transaction constitute fraud?
   A. If a reasonable person would attach decision-making importance to the omitted information
   B. Only if the information was known beyond all doubt to be factual
   C. Only in the case of a new issue of securities
   D. Any time the information is known by fewer than 25 persons

23. Under the Uniform Securities Act, all of the following are prohibited practices EXCEPT
   A. making recommendations on the basis of material, nonpublic information
   B. making recommendations on the basis of material information after that information has been publicly released
   C. making recommendations without having reasonable grounds for believing they are suitable
   D. stating that recommendations have been approved by the Administrator

24. Under the Uniform Securities Act, all of the following are prohibited business practices EXCEPT

    A. failing to indicate that securities prices are subject to market fluctuation
    B. ignoring an order to buy a stock immediately at the market price because the price is falling and the customer will likely get a better price by waiting
    C. telling a customer that commission, taxes, and other costs will be higher than normal even when you do not know exactly how high they will be
    D. wash sales and matching orders to create the appearance of market activity

25. Which of the following activities of an investment advisory firm would not require notification to and consent of the clients of that advisory firm?

    A. The retirement of a sole proprietor investment adviser wishing to sell the practice to another investment adviser
    B. The chief operating officer of an investment advisory firm wishing to pledge her majority interest in the firm to a local bank for a loan to purchase an office building that will be leased to the advisory firm
    C. A minority partner resigning from the firm to start his own advisory firm
    D. An investment adviser wishing to merge with a larger, national advisory firm

26. Which of the following investment advisory contracts would be lawful?

    I. An investment advisory contract for ABC Mutual Fund providing that the investment adviser will be paid 1% of the fund's net asset value as of the last business day of June and December
    II. An investment advisory contract providing that the adviser will receive 5% of any increase in the client's capital assets as of the end of each calendar year
    III. An investment advisory contract specifying that the investment adviser will receive 2% of the first $10,000 of profit and 1% of all profit over $10,000 in the client's account at the end of each quarter
    IV. An investment advisory contract providing that the adviser is to receive ½% of the monthly value of the funds in the client's account averaged over a 12-month period

    A. I and II
    B. I and IV
    C. I, II, III and IV
    D. None of the above

27. Making recommendations on the basis of material inside information about an issuer or its securities, when this information has not been made public, is prohibited. Therefore, an agent or broker/dealer doing which of the following would be engaging in a fraudulent practice?

    I. Giving inside information to privileged clients without a fee
    II. Informing other issuers about the inside information with the intent of collectively taking advantage of the information
    III. Having your relatives in another state invest heavily in this security when it appears in the market
    IV. Investing large sums of the firm's money in this issue with the written consent of all partners

    A. I and III
    B. I and IV
    C. II and IV
    D. I, II, III and IV

28. You have a wealthy client who complains to you about the extremely low rates currently being offered by his bank on CDs. You tell him that you are willing to borrow up to $100,000 for 2 years at prime +1 and will deposit securities you own as collateral. Under the Uniform Securities Act

    A. it is prohibited to borrow money from a client unless the client is in the money lending business
    B. it is always prohibited to pay a client more than a bank CD rate
    C. it could be permitted if the proper disclosures were made
    D. approval of the appropriate supervisor of your firm would be required

29. A client has a cash account at his broker/dealer. Now, he wishes to open a margin account as well. Which of the following best describes the action that must be taken?

    A. Verbal instructions to open the account are sufficient because the customer relationship already exists.
    B. The customer must make the request in writing, either by mail or by fax.
    C. The account may not be opened until the customer has completed and signed the margin account agreements.
    D. The customer must physically present himself at the agent's office and sign the appropriate papers.

30. Broker/dealer A wants to promote and reward teamwork. The firm plans to pay out a small percentage of year-end profits to the clerical staff as a bonus for their hard work. Under NASAA rules, is this permitted?

    A. Yes, if the bonuses are equally divided
    B. Yes, if all the agents agree to it
    C. Yes, if the clerical staff are all registered agents of the firm
    D. Yes, as long as the compensation is not sales related

ANSWERS AND RATIONALES

1. **C.** Front running, the practice of entering an order for the benefit of the firm ahead of a customer order, is a form of market manipulation. Matched trades or matched purchases occur when market participants agree to buy and sell securities among themselves to create the appearance of heightened market activity; this is also a form of market manipulation. Although churning is a prohibited practice, it does not involve manipulating the market, and arbitrage is the perfectly legal practice of buying a security in one marketplace and simultaneously selling it in another to benefit from a price disparity.

2. **C.** All other choices are clearly a misrepresentation of account status.

3. **D.** It is permissible to sell rights, which are securities. Borrowing money or securities from other than a bank or broker/dealer in the business of lending, failing to identify a customer's financial objectives, and guaranteeing a customer's account against losses are all prohibited practices.

4. **D.** Failure to bring customers' written complaints to the attention of the agent's broker/dealer is prohibited.

5. **D.** An Administrator may deny or revoke an agent's registration if the agent engages in prohibited practices such as those described in each of the choices in the question.

6. **C.** The Administrator may prohibit advisers from having custody of client funds or securities. If no such prohibition applies, the Administrator must be notified in writing if an adviser has custody. In almost all jurisdictions, a bond or sufficient net worth is required to maintain custody. Discretionary authority does not affect an adviser's ability to have custody.

7. **A.** Creating the illusion of trading activity is market manipulation. Guaranteeing performance of a security and omitting material facts are prohibited practices but do not constitute market manipulation. Trades too large for a customer are also prohibited because they are not suitable, but they are not market manipulation.

8. **A.** Federal registration is required of any investment adviser managing at least $30 million in assets. It is optional at $25 million; anything less requires state registration. The NSMIA provides that any investment adviser under contract to an investment company registered under the Investment Company Act of 1940 is required to register with the SEC as a federal covered adviser. Providing advice on federal covered securities listed on the NYSE does not make the adviser a federal covered adviser. Banks and their representatives are always excluded from the definition of investment adviser, federal covered or not.

9. **B.** An agent may not offer services that he cannot perform. An agent may participate actively in trading a security in which an unusually high trading volume has occurred, provided the trading is not designed to create a false appearance of high volume. At the client's request, an agent can alter a client's order, even if the change results in a loss. An agent is only required to report written complaints to his employing principal, although it would be wise to report repeated oral complaints.

10. **D.** The use of information that has no basis in fact, such as a rumor, is prohibited.

11. **C.** Agents must always determine suitability before soliciting purchases or sales. The key here is that the agent recommended this stock to all clients. One investment cannot be suitable for all of your clients.

12. **D.** All of the practices are prohibited. An agent may not borrow money or securities from a customer unless that customer is a bank or broker/dealer in the business of lending money and/or securities. Selling speculative or hot issues to a retired couple of modest means is an unsuitable transaction because it is not consistent with the objectives of the client. An agent must follow legal orders of the customer, even if the agent believes the order is an unwise one. An agent may not backdate confirmations for the benefit of the client.

13. **A.** An agent may indicate that a security is registered or is exempt from registration. All of the other statements are illegal.

14. **C.** Material facts are facts that an investor relies on to make investment decisions. The omission of a material fact in the sale, purchase, or offer of a security is fraudulent. This applies whether the security offered is exempt or nonexempt.

15. **B.** The function of the specialist is to act as a broker for orders that other broker/dealers left with him and to act as a dealer in buying and selling for his own account. His activity is not prohibited. Allowing a rumor to spread and then trading in response to it is a prohibited practice. Selling stock at the bid price and making up the difference with a personal check is a prohibited practice. Filling a firm's proprietary order ahead of a customer's order is a prohibited practice called front running.

16. **D.** Recommending tax shelters to low-income retirees is an example of an unsuitable transaction. Stating that an Administrator has approved an offering on the basis of the quality of information in the prospectus, soliciting orders for unregistered nonexempt securities, and employing a device to defraud are all prohibited practices under the USA.

17. **D.** As long as retaining custody of funds is not prohibited, an investment adviser may have custody of a customer's account after providing notice to the Administrator.

18. **A.** It is a prohibited practice under the USA for an agent to share in the profits or losses of a customer's account unless the customer and the employer have given written consent and the percentage of participation is proportionate to the percentage of the agent's personal funds in the account. An agent is permitted to jointly own a personal account at the firm and can refuse to share in a customer's account.

19. **D.** The rules regarding investment advisers and account trading are much more strict than those for broker/dealers because of the fiduciary responsibility of the adviser. Any action that results in a transaction in which the firm or an affiliate acts in either a principal or agency capacity requires written disclosure of that fact to the client and prior approval of the client.

20. **A.** Any change in the ownership of an investment advisory firm organized as a partnership, no matter how small, requires notification to all clients within a reasonable amount of time. If the firm is structured as a corporation, pledging a controlling interest in the company's stock is viewed as an assignment of the contracts. This may not be done without the approval of the clients. Agency cross transactions (i.e., transactions in which the adviser represents both sides of the trade) are permitted as long as the adviser makes the proper written disclosures and does not make buy/sell recommendations to either party.

21. **B.** Although Raymond is certainly in trouble and may have his registration revoked or suspended, the firm may also have problems. First, the Administrator may close the firm because of inadequate capital. It is also possible that the firm may face disciplinary action because of failure to properly supervise Raymond. An agent cannot be an

agent without representing a dealer, so this action would automatically terminate the licenses of all the agents who work for this firm.

22. **A.** It is illegal to intentionally omit a material fact that should have been disclosed to a customer. The definition includes the criterion of whether a reasonable person would attach decision-making importance to the omitted information to fully define the term *material fact*.

23. **B.** Nonpublic (inside) information of a material nature never may be used. All recommendations must be suitable, and recommendations are never approved by the Administrator.

24. **C.** It is appropriate to tell a customer that certain costs will be higher than normal, even if it is not known how much higher. In fact, it would be a prohibited practice to fail to inform the customer of such higher costs before the trade. All of the other choices are prohibited actions.

25. **C.** If the firm is a partnership, any change to a minority interest in that partnership requires notification to all clients within a reasonable period. Consent is required only before an assignment of the client's contract. All of the other choices meet the act's definition of *assignment*.

26. **B.** An investment adviser may not be compensated on the basis of capital gains in the client's account. Compensation may be based on a percentage rate of the average assets taken over a certain period.

27. **D.** All the answer choices involve fraudulent trading in response to insider information. Material information not available to the investing public cannot be used by anyone when making investment decisions.

28. **A.** You can never borrow money from a client who is not in the money lending business.

29. **C.** Opening a margin account is far more detailed than opening a cash account. There are a number of different agreements that have to be signed. The presence of an existing cash account is meaningless here, and a verbal or written request to open an account accomplishes nothing.

30. **D.** NASAA rules permit bonuses to nonregistered personnel as long as the compensation is not directly tied to sales of securities.

QUICK QUIZ ANSWERS

Quick Quiz 3.1

1. **U.** It is unlawful to guarantee the performance of any security. Even though the government securities are guaranteed, the mutual fund investment is not.

2. **U.** It is unlawful to exercise discretion without prior written authorization. Because the client was a nondiscretionary client, the agent could not, on his own initiative, select which Internet company to invest in.

3. **L.** An agent must refuse orders from anyone other than the customer unless that person has prior written trading authority.

4. **U.** All written customer complaints must be forwarded to a principal of the agent's employing broker/dealer.

5. **L.** Agents may borrow from banks or financial institutions that are in the business of lending money to public customers. Agents may not borrow money from customers who are not in the business of lending money.

6. **U.** An agent may not guarantee the performance of a security.

7. **L.** It is lawful to charge extra transaction fees when justified as long as the customer is informed before the transaction.

8. **U.** It is unlawful to promise services that an agent cannot reasonably expect to perform or that the agent is not qualified to perform.

9. **U.** It is unlawful to solicit unregistered nonexempt securities.

Quick Quiz 3.2

1. **A.** Material disciplinary violations must be reported by all investment advisers, regardless of whether they keep custody. The first 2 answers fit the definition of material actions, but not the third. If the suit goes in favor of the client and the adviser is found guilty, disclosure would need to be made.

Quick Quiz 3.3

1. **C.** The USA does not require investment advisers to include in their contracts a list of states in which they are licensed to do business. The USA does require advisers to include their method of computing fees, a statement prohibiting assignment without client consent, and notification of change in membership of the investment partnership.

2. **F.** An Administrator may, by rule or order, prevent an adviser from taking custody. If an Administrator prevents custody, an adviser cannot overrule the Administrator by notifying the Administrator first.

3. **F.** An adviser may sell securities to clients from its own account provided disclosure is made upon receipt of written consent from the client before executing the trade.

4. **T.** Investment advisers are bound by the regulations that apply to sales activities as well as those that apply to advisory activities. The reverse is also true. When a sales agent engages in investment advisory activities, the agent is bound by the rules that apply to providing investment advice to others as well as those that apply to sales practices.

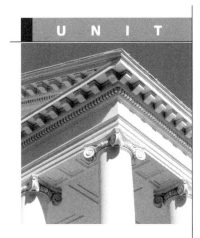

4

The Administrative Provisions of the Uniform Securities Act

The USA is model legislation for the states to use in writing their own securities laws. On your exam, you will not be tested on the specifics of your state's securities laws but on the principles of state regulation laid out in the USA.

This Unit addresses the administrative provisions of the act. Under the USA, the state Administrator has jurisdiction over securities transactions that originate in, are directed into, or are accepted in the Administrator's state.

When a securities transaction falls within the Administrator's jurisdiction, the Administrator has power to make rules and orders; conduct investigations and issue subpoenas; issue cease and desist orders; and deny, suspend, or revoke registrations.

Both civil liabilities and criminal penalties exist for violating the act.

The Series 63 exam will include six questions on the material presented in this Unit. ■

When you have completed this Unit, you should be able to:

■ **describe** the relationship between state and national securities laws;

■ **recognize** the jurisdiction of the state securities Administrator;

■ **list** the powers of the Administrator within his jurisdiction;

■ **describe** the rights of recovery for a security's sale or for investment advice purchased in violation of the USA; and

■ **contrast** civil and criminal penalties for violation of the act.

JURISDICTION AND POWERS OF THE STATE ADMINISTRATOR

The jurisdiction and powers of the Administrator extend to activities related to securities transactions originated in, directed to, and accepted in the state.

SALE OR SELL AND OFFER OR OFFER TO SELL

Sale or Sell

The USA defines **sale** or **sell** as every contract of sale, contract to sell, and disposition of a security or interest in a security for value. This means that any transfer of a security in which money or some other valuable consideration is involved is covered by this definition and subject to the act.

Offer or Offer to Sell

The USA defines **offer** or **offer to sell** as every attempt or offer to dispose of, or solicitation of an offer to buy, a security or interest in a security for value. These terms include any:

■   security given or delivered with, or as a bonus on account of, any purchase of securities or other items constituting part of the purchase;

■   gift of assessable stock (assessable stock is stock issued below par for which the issuer or creditors have the right to assess shareholders for the balance of unpaid par); or

■   warrant or right to purchase or subscribe to another security (an offer of the other security is considered to be included in the warrant or right).

TAKE NOTE   You must be able to distinguish between a sale and an offer to sell. The offer is the attempt; a transaction has not taken place. In a sale, there has been an actual transaction involving money or another form of consideration for value. One must be properly registered to both make a sale and make the offer.

EXAMPLE   If a car dealer, as an essential part of a sale, offers $1,000 in corporate bonds as an incentive, this would be considered a bonus under the act; therefore, this sale falls under the jurisdiction of the state securities Administrator. As a result, to do this, the car dealer would have to register with the state as a broker/dealer.

When assessable stock is given as a gift, the Administrator has jurisdiction over the transaction because there is a potential future obligation in that either the issuer or, more likely, creditors can demand payment for the balance of the par value.

If an individual owned assessable stock and felt that the issuer was on the verge of bankruptcy, that person could give the stock as a present. If the bankruptcy occurred, the new owner would then be subject to the assessment.

TEST TOPIC ALERT   Assessable stock no longer exists, but the exam may ask about it.

The terms *offer* and *offer to sell* do not include any:

- bona fide pledge or loan;

- gift of nonassessable stock;

- stock dividend or stock split, if nothing of value is given by the stockholders for the additional shares;

- class vote by stockholders, pursuant to the certificate of incorporation or the applicable corporation statute, or a merger, consolidation, reclassification of securities, or sale of corporate assets in consideration of the issuance of securities of another corporation; or

- act incidental to a judicially approved reorganization with which a security is issued in exchange for one or more outstanding securities, claims, or property interest, or partly in such exchange and partly for cash.

JURISDICTION OF THE ADMINISTRATOR

Under law, for any agent of a state (e.g., the Administrator) to have authority over an activity such as a sale or offer of securities, he must have legal jurisdiction to act. Jurisdiction under the USA specifically means the legal authority to regulate securities activities that take place in the state.

The USA describes activities considered to have taken place in the state as any offer to buy or sell a security, as well as any acceptance of the offer, if the offer:

- originated in the Administrator's state;

- is directed to the Administrator's state; or

- is accepted in the Administrator's state.

TAKE NOTE   Because securities transactions often involve several states, more than one Administrator may have jurisdiction over a security or a transaction.

CASE STUDY

Offer Originated in Administrator's State

Situation: Mr. Thompson (a registered agent in Illinois), on the recommendation of his best client (Mr. Bixby), phones a friend of Mr. Bixby's in Indiana. Mr. Thompson sells a security to Mr. Bixby's friend, Ms. Gordon, who then mails payment to Mr. Thompson's office in Illinois.

Analysis: The Administrators of both Illinois and Indiana have jurisdiction—the Administrator of Illinois has jurisdiction because the call (offer) originated in Illinois, and the Administrator of Indiana has jurisdiction because the offer was accepted by Ms. Gordon in Indiana.

CASE STUDY

Offer Directed to Administrator's State

Situation: The day after he completes his first transaction with Ms. Gordon, Mr. Thompson mails sales offering materials to her home address in Indiana. Ms. Gordon is not in a position to buy more securities, so she discards the material without reading it.

Analysis: By sending sales materials to Ms. Gordon's home address in Indiana, Mr. Thompson directed the offer to Indiana. Even though Ms. Gordon discarded the information, the Administrator in Indiana has jurisdiction because the sales offer was directed to Indiana. The Administrator of Illinois also has jurisdiction because the offer originated in Illinois.

CASE STUDY

Offer Accepted in Administrator's State

Situation: Mr. Thompson sends additional offers to Ms. Gordon in Indiana, who is now on a three-month summer vacation in Florida. Ms. Gordon has her mail forwarded to her in Florida. Upon receiving Mr. Thompson's materials in Florida, she decides to purchase the securities. She pays for the securities by mailing a check to Mr. Thompson drawn from her local bank in Indiana.

Analysis: The offer was accepted by Ms. Gordon while she was in Florida; therefore, the Administrator of Florida has jurisdiction. Additionally, the Administrator in Illinois has jurisdiction because the offer originated in Illinois, and the Administrator in Indiana has jurisdiction because the offer was directed to Indiana. This is a situation where the Administrators of three different states have jurisdiction.

PUBLISHING AND BROADCAST EXCEPTIONS TO JURISDICTION

There are special rules regarding the Administrator's jurisdiction over offers made through a TV or radio broadcast or a bona fide newspaper.

The Administrator would not have jurisdiction if the offer were made under any of the following circumstances:

- Television or radio broadcast that originated outside of the state

- Bona fide newspaper or periodical published outside of the state

■ Newspaper or periodical published inside the state that has more than two-thirds (66%) of its circulation outside the state in the last year

---

TAKE NOTE

A bona fide newspaper is a newspaper of general interest and circulation, such as *The New York Times*. Private investment advisory newsletters, usually distributed by subscription, are not bona fide newspapers and therefore are not included in the publishing exception.

CASE STUDY

Publishing and Broadcast Exemptions

Situation: First Securities & Co., broker/dealers with offices in New York state and Illinois, offers to sell shares in a new retail shoe store chain located in New York. First Securities advertises the offering to residents of New York in the local newspaper, the *New York Gazette*. First Securities also advertises through the *Gazette's* wholly owned radio station. The *Gazette* and its radio station are located in western New York near the Pennsylvania border. About 55% of the *Gazette's* readers and listeners live in Pennsylvania.

Analysis: Although more than half the readers and listeners of the *Gazette* live in Pennsylvania, under the terms of the publishing and broadcasting exemption of the USA, the offer is not made in Pennsylvania because the paper is not published in Pennsylvania. Therefore, the Administrator of New York state has sole jurisdiction over the offering. No dual or multiple jurisdiction applies in this case, unless the offer is actually accepted in Pennsylvania. The fact that First Securities is registered in Illinois in addition to New York is not relevant to this offering because no securities were sold there, nor were any offers or advertising directed to the state.

QUICK QUIZ 4.1

1. A state's securities Administrator has jurisdiction over a securities offering if it
   A. was directed to residents of that state
   B. was originated in that state
   C. was accepted in that state
   D. all of the above

2. An Administrator has jurisdiction over an offer to sell securities if it is made in a newspaper published within the state with no more than
   A. ⅓ of its circulation outside the state
   B. ½ of its circulation outside the state
   C. ⅔ of its circulation outside the state
   D. 90% of its circulation outside the state

Quick Quiz answers can be found at the end of the Unit.

POWERS OF THE ADMINISTRATOR WITHIN ITS JURISDICTION

The USA not only establishes the jurisdiction of the Administrator but also outlines the powers or the actions that the Administrator can take within its jurisdiction.

The four broad powers the Administrator has to enforce and administer the act in his state are to:

- make, amend, or rescind rules and orders;

- conduct investigations and issue subpoenas;

- issue cease and desist orders and seek injunctions; and

- deny, suspend, cancel, or revoke registrations and licenses.

Although the Administrator has powers to enforce the act for the benefit of the public, the Administrator, as well as his employees, have an obligation not to use the office for personal gain. Administrators are, as a result, prohibited from using, for their own benefit, any information derived from their official duties that has not been made public.

MAKE, AMEND, OR RESCIND RULES AND ORDERS

To enforce the USA, the Administrator has the authority to make, amend, or rescind rules and orders necessary to administer the act. The Administrator may also issue interpretive letters. The USA requires that all rules and orders be published. A rule or order of the Administrator has the same authority as a provision of the act itself, but these rules and orders are not part of the USA itself. The difference between a rule and an order is that a rule applies to everyone, whereas an order applies to a specific instance.

 EXAMPLE

The Administrator may decide to issue a rule requiring all agents to pay an annual registration fee of $250. This rule applies to everyone. Or, the Administrator may find that a specific agent has violated a provision of the law and orders a 30-day suspension. This order applies only to that particular agent.

A person may challenge an order of the Administrator in court within 60 days of order issuance.

Although the Administrator has the power to make and amend rules for compliance with his state's blue-sky law, he does not have the power to alter the law itself.

The composition or content of state securities law is the responsibility of the state legislature, not of administrative agencies. Rules for administration and compliance with the law are the responsibility of the securities Administrator.

CASE STUDY   **Rules and Orders of the Administrator**

Situation: The Iowa state securities Administrator requires, by rule, that all companies registering their securities in Iowa must supply financial statements in a specific form and with content prescribed by the Administrator. However, the Administrator does not publish the rule because the rule is too long and complex.

Analysis: The USA allows state Administrators to issue rules and orders in carrying out their regulatory functions, and the Iowa Administrator acted properly in designing the form and content for financial reports. However, the USA requires that Administrators publish all rules and orders. The Administrator, despite the latitude he has in administering the USA, cannot suspend any provision of the USA itself. The Iowa Administrator acted within his authority in designing the forms but acted without authority (i.e., he violated the USA) in suspending the requirement that all rules and orders be published.

CONDUCT INVESTIGATIONS AND ISSUE SUBPOENAS

The Administrator has broad discretionary authority to conduct investigations and issue subpoenas. These investigations may be made in public or in private and may occur within or outside of the Administrator's state. Normally, these investigations are open to the public, but when, in the opinion of the Administrator and with the consent of all parties, it is felt that a private investigation is more appropriate, that investigation will be conducted without public scrutiny.

In conducting an investigation, the Administrator, or any officer designated by him, has the power to:

■ require statements in writing, under oath, regarding all matters relating to the issue under investigation;

■ publish and make public the facts and circumstances concerning the issue to be investigated;

■ subpoena witnesses and compel their attendance and testimony; and

■ take evidence and require the production of books, papers, correspondence, and any other documents deemed relevant.

TAKE NOTE   In addition to having the power to conduct investigations, the Administrator may enforce subpoenas issued by Administrators in other states on the same basis as if the alleged offense took place in the Administrator's state.

ISSUE CEASE AND DESIST ORDERS

If an Administrator determines that a person is about to engage in an activity that constitutes a violation of the USA, the Administrator may issue a cease and desist order without a hearing. The Administrator is granted this power to prevent potential violations before they occur.

Although the Administrator has the power to issue cease and desist orders, he does not have the legal power to compel compliance with the order. To compel compliance in the face of a person's resistance, the Administrator must apply to a court of competent jurisdiction for an injunction. Only the courts can compel compliance by issuing injunctions and imposing penalties for violation of them. If a temporary or permanent injunction is issued, upon request of the Administrator, a receiver or conservator may be appointed over the defendant's assets.

TAKE NOTE   Cease and desist orders are not the same as stop orders. Cease and desist orders are directed to persons, requiring them to cease activities. Stop orders are directed to registration applications.

CASE STUDY   **Cease and Desist Orders**

Situation: Mr. Thompson is registered to conduct business in the state of Illinois and makes plans to sell a security within the next few days. The Administrator considers this security ineligible for sale in the state. The Administrator orders Mr. Thompson to stop his sales procedures immediately.

Analysis: The Administrator of Illinois issued a cease and desist order to Mr. Thompson because there was not sufficient time to conduct a public hearing before the sale to determine whether the security was eligible for sale in the state.

Frequently, before a final determination of proceedings under the act, the Administrator will act summarily to suspend a registration. However, no formal order may be issued without the Administrator:

- giving appropriate prior notice to the affected persons;

- granting an opportunity for a hearing; and

- providing findings of fact and conclusions of law.

DENY, SUSPEND, CANCEL, OR REVOKE REGISTRATIONS

The Administrator also has the power to deny, suspend, cancel, or revoke the registration of broker/dealers, investment advisers, and their representatives, as well as the registration of securities issues.

Broker/Dealers, Advisers, and Their Representatives

To justify a denial, revocation, or suspension of the license of a securities professional, the Administrator must find that the order is in the public interest and also find that the applicant or registrant, or in the case of a broker/dealer or investment adviser, any partner, officer, or director, or any person occupying a similar status or performing similar functions:

- has filed an incomplete, false, or misleading registration application;

- has willfully violated the USA;

- has been convicted of a securities-related misdemeanor within the last 10 years;

- has been convicted of any felony within the last 10 years;

- has been enjoined by law from engaging in the securities business;

- is subject to an Administrator's denial, revocation, or suspension;

- is engaged in dishonest or unethical securities practices;

- is insolvent (this does not apply to agents or investment adviser representatives);

- has failed to pay application filing fees; or

- is not qualified because of lack of training, experience, or knowledge of the securities business.

TAKE NOTE   The public's best interest is not reason enough for the denial, suspension, or revocation of a registration. There must be an additional reason.

The Administrator must notify the registrant of any reason to deny, suspend, revoke, or cancel a registration and, if asked in writing, must provide a hearing within 15 days. The Administrator may not stop a registration on the basis of facts that were known to the Administrator at the time the registration became effective (unless the proceedings are initiated within 30 days).

Securities Issues

As is the case with a securities professional, a securities Administrator may deny, suspend, cancel, or revoke a security's registration if the order is in the public's interest and the securities registrant:

- files a misleading or incomplete registration statement;

- is engaged in an offering that is fraudulent or made on unfair, unjust, or inequitable terms;

- charges offering fees that are excessive or unreasonable;

- has a control person convicted of a securities-related crime;

- is subject to a court injunction; or

■   is engaged in a method of business that is illegal.

In addition, the Administrator may deny a registration if the applicant fails to pay the filing fee. When the fee is paid, the denial order will be removed, provided the applicant is in compliance with all registration procedures.

QUICK QUIZ 4.2

1. With regard to the powers of the Administrator, which of the following statements are NOT true?
    I.   The Administrator must seek an injunction to issue a cease and desist order.
    II.   The USA requires an Administrator to conduct a full hearing, public or private, before issuing a cease and desist order.
    III. The USA grants the Administrator the power to issue injunctions to force compliance with the provisions of the act.
    A.   I and II
    B.   I and III
    C.   II and III
    D.   I, II and III

2. Although the Administrator has great power, the USA does place some limitations on the office. Which of the following statements regarding those powers are TRUE?
    I.   In conducting an investigation, an Administrator can compel the testimony of witnesses.
    II.   Investigations of serious violations must be open to the public.
    III. An Administrator in Illinois may enforce subpoenas from South Carolina only if the violation originally occurred in Illinois.
    IV.   An Administrator may deny the registration of a securities professional who has been convicted of a felony within the past 10 years but must provide, if requested in writing, a hearing within 15 days.
    A.   I, II and IV
    B.   I, III and IV
    C.   I and IV
    D.   II and III

NONPUNITIVE TERMINATIONS OF REGISTRATION

A registration can be terminated even if there has not been a violation of the USA. A request for withdrawal and lack of qualification are both reasons for cancellation.

Withdrawal

A person may request on his own initiative a withdrawal of a registration. The withdrawal is effective 30 days after the Administrator receives it, provided no revocation or suspension proceedings are in process against the person making the request. In that event, the Administrator may institute a revocation or suspension proceeding within one year after a withdrawal becomes effective.

Lack of Qualification

An Administrator may not base a denial of a person's registration solely on his lack of experience. However, the Administrator may consider that registration as a broker/dealer does not necessarily qualify one for a license as an investment adviser and may restrict that applicant's registration as a broker/dealer conditional upon its not functioning as an investment adviser.

Cancellation

If an Administrator finds that an applicant or a registrant no longer exists or has ceased to transact business, the Administrator may cancel the registration.

TEST TOPIC ALERT

You may encounter this type of question regarding cancellation: "What would the Administrator do if mailings to a registrant were returned with no forwarding address?" The answer is, "Cancel the registration."

The Administrator may also cancel a registration if a person is declared mentally incompetent.

TAKE NOTE

Be familiar with the distinction between cancellation and denial, suspension, or revocation. Cancellation does not result from violations or a failure to follow the provisions of the act. Cancellation occurs as the result of death, dissolution, or mental incompetency.

QUICK QUIZ 4.3

1. Which of the following statements relating to termination of registration is TRUE?
   A. A registration, once in effect, may never be voluntarily withdrawn.
   B. An Administrator may not cancel a registration of a securities professional who is declared mentally incompetent.
   C. An Administrator may revoke the registration of a securities professional who is declared mentally incompetent.
   D. An Administrator may cancel the registration of a registrant no longer in business.

PENALTIES FOR VIOLATIONS OF THE UNIFORM SECURITIES ACT

The USA provides both civil liabilities and criminal penalties for persons who violate the USA. In addition, the act provides for recovery by a client of financial loss that results from the fraudulent sale of a security or investment advice.

CIVIL LIABILITIES

Persons who sell securities or offer investment advice in violation of the USA are subject to civil liabilities (as well as criminal penalties).

The purchaser of securities sold in violation of the act may sue the seller to recover financial loss.

The purchaser can sue for recovery if the:

- securities were sold in violation of the registration provisions of the USA;

- securities professional omitted or made an untrue statement of material fact;

- securities were sold by an agent who should have been but was not registered under the act; or

- securities were sold in violation of a rule or order of the securities Administrator.

Statute of Limitations

The time limit, or **statute of limitations**, for violations of the civil provisions of the USA is three years from the date of sale (or rendering of investment advice) or two years after discovering the violation, whichever occurred first.

Rights of Recovery from Improper Sale of Securities

If the seller of securities discovers that he has made a sale in violation of the USA, the seller may offer to repurchase the securities from the buyer. In this case, the seller is offering the buyer the **right of rescission**. To satisfy the buyer's right of rescission, the amount paid back to the buyer must include the original purchase price and interest as determined by the Administrator.

By offering to buy back the securities that were sold in violation of the act, the seller can avoid a lawsuit through a **letter of rescission**. The buyer has 30 days after receiving the letter of rescission to respond. If the buyer does not accept or reject the rescission offer within 30 days, the buyer forfeits the right to pursue a lawsuit at a later date.

If the buyer accepts the rescission offer, he may recover:

- the original purchase price of the securities;

- plus interest at a rate determined by the Administrator;

- plus all reasonable attorney's fees;

- minus income received during the period in which the securities were held.

Rights of Recovery from Improper Investment Advice

A person who buys a security as the result of investment advice received in violation of the USA also has the right of rescission. In the case of securities purchased as a result of improper investment advice, the buyer may recover:

- the cost of the advice;
- plus losses resulting from the advice;
- plus all interest costs from the date of fee payment at a rate determined by the Administrator;
- plus any reasonable attorney's fees.

TAKE NOTE
When securities are sold improperly, the buyer can recover the original purchase price in addition to other losses. When improper investment advice is offered, the purchaser of the advice is entitled to recover the cost of the advice and losses incurred but is not entitled to recover the original purchase price from the adviser.

CRIMINAL PENALTIES

Persons found guilty of a fraudulent securities transaction are subject to criminal penalties (as well as civil liabilities). Upon conviction, a person may be fined, imprisoned, or both. To be convicted of fraud, the violation must be willful and the registrant must know that the activity is fraudulent.

TAKE NOTE
Fraud is the deliberate or willful concealment, misrepresentation, or omission of material information or the truth to deceive or manipulate another person for unlawful or unfair gain. Under the USA, fraud is not limited to common-law deceit.

Statute of Limitations

The statute of limitations for criminal offenses under the USA is five years from the date of the offense.

TAKE NOTE
Remember the sequence 5-5-3 for the application of criminal penalties: 5-year statute of limitations, $5,000 maximum fine, and imprisonment of no more than 3 years.

Under the civil provisions, the statute of limitations is 2 years from the discovery of the offense or 3 years after the act occurred, whichever occurs first.

CASE STUDY
Fraudulent Sale of Securities

Situation: Mr. Thompson, the registered sales agent, knowingly omitted the fact that the shares of a company he sold to his client, Mr. Bixby, were downgraded to speculative grade and that their bonds were placed on a credit watch by one of the major credit rating agencies. A month after the sale, the shares became worthless.

Analysis: Mr. Thompson sold these securities to Mr. Bixby in violation of the USA because he deliberately or knowingly failed to mention material information—information that was important for Mr. Bixby to know to make an informed investment decision. Mr. Bixby has the right to recover the financial losses that resulted from the sale.

TAKE NOTE   Under the USA, the actual seller of the securities or the advice is not the only person liable for the violation of the act. Every person who directly or indirectly controls the person who sold the securities or the advice, or is a material aid to the transaction, is also liable to the same extent as the person who conducted the transaction.

JUDICIAL REVIEW OF ORDERS (APPEAL)

Any person affected by an order of the Administrator may obtain a review of the order in an appropriate court by filing a written petition within 60 days. In general, filing an appeal does not automatically act as a stay of the penalty. The order will go into effect as issued unless the court rules otherwise.

QUICK QUIZ 4.4
1. Which of the following statements relating to penalties under the USA is TRUE?
   A. Unknowing violation of the USA by an agent is cause for imprisonment under the criminal liability provisions of the act.
   B. If a violation has occurred in the sale of a security, the purchaser of the security may recover the original purchase price, legal costs, and interest, less any earnings already received.
   C. A seller who notices that a sale was made in violation of the act may offer a right of rescission to the purchaser; the purchaser must accept this right within the earlier of two years after notice of the violation or three years after the sale.
   D. Any person aggrieved by an order of the Administrator may request an appeal of the order within 15 days which, in effect, functions as a stay of the order during the appeal period.

HOTSHEETS

For your convenience, Unit HotSheets summarizing the key points are located at the end of the manual on perforated pages.

UNIT TEST

1. If convicted of a willful violation of the Uniform Securities Act, an agent is subject to

   A. imprisonment for 5 years
   B. a fine of $5,000 and/or imprisonment for 3 years
   C. a fine of $10,000
   D. disbarment

2. To protect the public, the Administrator may

   I. deny a registration if the registrant does not have sufficient experience to function as an agent
   II. limit a registrant's functions to those of a broker/dealer if, in the initial application for registration as an investment adviser, the registrant is not qualified to act as an adviser
   III. take into consideration in approving a registration that the registrant will work under the supervision of a registered investment adviser or broker/dealer
   IV. deny a registration, although denial is not in the public's interest, if it is prudent in view of a change in the state's political composition

   A. I and II
   B. II and III
   C. III and IV
   D. I, II, III and IV

3. Aaron is a client of XYZ Financial Services. Over the past several years, Aaron has been suspicious of possible churning of his account but has taken no action because account performance has been outstanding. After reviewing his most recent statement, Aaron suspects that excessive transactions have occurred. He consults his attorney, who informs him that under the USA, any lawsuit for recovery of damages under the USA must be started within

   A. 1 year of occurrence
   B. 2 years of occurrence
   C. 3 years of occurrence or 2 years of discovery, whichever occurs first
   D. 2 years of occurrence or 3 years of discovery, whichever occurs last

4. Which of the following accurately describes a cease and desist order as authorized by the USA?

   A. An order that a federal agency issued to a brokerage firm to stop an advertising campaign
   B. An Administrator's order to refrain from a practice of business he believes to be unfair
   C. A court-issued order requiring a business to stop an unfair practice
   D. An order from one brokerage firm to another to refrain from unfair business practices

5. A customer living in one state receives a phone call from an agent in another state. A transaction between the two occurs in yet another state. According to the Uniform Securities Act, under whose jurisdiction does the transaction fall?

   A. Administrator of the state in which the customer lives
   B. Administrator of the state from which the agent made the call
   C. Administrator of the state in which the transaction took place
   D. Administrators of all 3 states involved

6. By rule, the Administrator may

   A. forbid an adviser from taking custody of client funds
   B. allow an agent to waive provisions of the USA
   C. suspend federal law if he believes it to be in the public interest
   D. suspend the registration of a federal covered adviser because the contract did not meet the requirements for a state-sanctioned investment advisory contract

7. If it is in the public interest, the Uniform Securities Act provides that the state Administrator may deny the registration of a broker/dealer for all of the following reasons EXCEPT

   A. the applicant is not qualified because of lack of experience
   B. a willful violation of the Uniform Securities Act has taken place
   C. the applicant is financially insolvent
   D. the applicant is enjoined temporarily from engaging in the securities business

8. If an agent chooses to appeal an Administrator's order, when must the agent file for review of the order with the appropriate court?

   A. Immediately
   B. Within 30 days after the entry of the order
   C. Within 60 days after the entry of the order
   D. Within 180 days after the entry of the order

9. An Administrator may summarily suspend a registration pending final determination of proceedings under the USA. However, the Administrator may not enter an order without

   I. appropriate prior notice to the applicant as well as the employer or prospective employer of the applicant
   II. opportunity for a hearing
   III. findings of fact and conclusions of law
   IV. prior written acknowledgment of the applicant
   A. I only
   B. I and II
   C. I, II and III
   D. I, II, III and IV

10. The Administrator has authority to

    I. issue a cease and desist order without a hearing
    II. issue a cease and desist order only after a hearing
    III. suspend a securities registration upon discovering an officer of the registrant has been convicted of a nonsecurities-related crime
    IV. sentence violators of the USA to 3 years in prison
    A. I only
    B. I and IV
    C. II and III
    D. II and IV

11. Which of the following statements regarding NASAA Guidelines is NOT true?

    A. The Administrator's rules apply to general situations.
    B. The Administrator's orders apply to specific situations.
    C. The Administrator may work in concert with the SEC in developing rules and regulations.
    D. At least once every 5 years, the Administrator's rules are subject to a relevancy review.

12. An agent lives in Montana and is registered in Montana and Idaho. His broker/dealer is registered in every state west of the Mississippi River. The agent's client, who lives in Montana, decides to enroll in a 1-year resident MBA program in Philadelphia. During the 1-year period when the client is in Philadelphia, the agent may

    A. conduct business with the client as usual
    B. only accept unsolicited orders
    C. not conduct business with the client
    D. not deal with the client until the broker/dealer registers in Pennsylvania

13. An Administrator may deny an investment adviser representative for all of the following reasons EXCEPT
    A. lack of experience
    B. failure to post a surety bond
    C. failure to pass a written exam
    D. not meeting minimum financial standards

14. The Administrator may cancel the registration of an adviser if
    A. mail is returned with a notice that the forwarding notice has expired
    B. the adviser is not in the business any longer
    C. a court has declared the adviser to be mentally incompetent
    D. any of the above

15. Currency transaction reports must be filed for cash transactions that exceed
    A. $10,000
    B. $25,000
    C. $50,000
    D. $100,000

A N S W E R S   A N D   R A T I O N A L E S

1. **B.**   Under the USA, the maximum penalty is a fine of $5,000 and/or 3 years in jail.

2. **B.**   The Administrator can deny, suspend, or revoke a registration for many reasons, but they must be in the interest of the public. The Administrator may not deny the registration simply because it is prudent. The Administrator may determine that an applicant, in his initial application for registration as an investment adviser, is not qualified to act as an adviser and thus may limit the registration to that of a broker/dealer; the Administrator can also take into consideration whether the registrant will work under the supervision of a registered investment adviser or broker/dealer when approving an application. Lack of experience is insufficient for denial.

3. **C.**   Under the USA, the lawsuit for recovery of damages must commence within the sooner of 3 years of occurrence of the offense or 2 years of its discovery.

4. **B.**   A cease and desist order is a directive from an administrative agency to immediately stop a particular action. Administrators may issue cease and desist orders with or without a hearing. Brokerage houses cannot issue cease and desist orders to each other.

5. **D.**   Under the scope of the Uniform Securities Act, if any part of a transaction occurs in a state, the transaction falls under the jurisdiction of the state Administrator. The transaction is under the control of the Administrator of the state in which the customer lives (because the offer was received there), the Administrator of the state in which the agent is calling (because the offer was made from that state), and the Administrator of the state in which the transaction took place.

6. **A.**   The Administrator has considerable discretion to make rules or issue orders. Specifically, the USA allows the Administrator to prohibit custody by rule. However, the USA does not allow the Administrator to waive provisions of the USA, nor can the Administrator suspend federal law.

7. **A.**   If the broker/dealer qualifies by virtue of training or knowledge, registration cannot be denied for lack of experience only. Registration may be denied if the applicant willfully violates the Uniform Securities Act, is financially insolvent, or has been enjoined from engaging in the securities business.

8. **C.**   Under the USA, a registered person has up to 60 days to appeal any disciplinary finding by the state Administrator.

9. **C.**   With the exception of proceedings awaiting final determination, the Administrator must provide appropriate prior notice to the applicant as well as the employer or prospective employer of the applicant and provide the opportunity for a hearing. In addition, the Administrator may issue a final stop order only after findings of fact and conclusions of law. An applicant is not required to provide written acknowledgment before an order is issued.

10. **A.**   The Administrator may issue a cease and desist order without a hearing but does not have the authority to sentence violators of the USA. The Administrator may not suspend a security's registration upon discovering, in subsequent years, that an officer of the firm has been convicted of a nonsecurities-related crime.

11. **D.**   Relevancy review is not part of the act.

12. **A.** Even though the college program is referred to as a resident program, that does not mean the client has changed his state of residence. Although neither the firm nor the agent is registered, the agent may continue to conduct business with the client because both the agent and his firm are properly registered in the client's state of permanent residence.

13. **A.** Lack of experience, by itself, is not cause for registration denial.

14. **D.** You must know the difference between cancellation of a registration (which requires no hearing) and revocation (which does).

15. **A.** The Bank Secrecy Act requires every financial institution to file a Currency Transaction Report (CTR) on FinCEN Form 104 for each cash transaction that exceeds $10,000. This report would include cash transactions used to pay off loans, electronic transfers of funds, and cash purchases of certificates of deposit, stocks, bonds, mutual funds, or other investments.

QUICK QUIZ ANSWERS

Quick Quiz 4.1

1. **D.** The Administrator has jurisdiction over a security offering if it was directed to, originated in, or was accepted in that state.

2. **C.** A state Administrator has jurisdiction over a securities offering made in a bona fide newspaper published within the state with no more than ⅔ of its circulation outside the state.

Quick Quiz 4.2

1. **D.** The Administrator need not seek an injunction to issue a cease and desist order. The USA does not require that an Administrator conduct a public or private hearing before issuing a cease and desist order. When time does not permit, the Administrator may issue a cease and desist order before a hearing to prevent a pending violation. The USA does not grant the Administrator the power to issue injunctions to force compliance with the act. The act permits the Administrator to issue cease and desist orders, and, if they do not work, the Administrator may seek an injunction from a court of competent jurisdiction. A cease and desist order is an administrative order, whereas an injunction is a judicial order.

2. **C.** An Administrator can compel the testimony of witnesses when conducting an investigation. Investigation of serious violations need not be held in public. An Administrator in Illinois may enforce subpoenas from South Carolina whether the violation occurred in Illinois or not. Conviction for any felony within the past 10 years is one of a number of reasons the Administrator has for denying a license. However, upon notice of the denial, a written request may be made for a hearing. That request must be honored within 15 days.

Quick Quiz 4.3

1. **D.** An administrator may cancel the registration of a registrant that is no longer in existence. A person may request a withdrawal of a registration. Withdrawals become effective after 30 days if there are no revocation or denial proceedings in process. An Administrator does not revoke the registration of a person who is declared mentally incompetent but cancels such registration; cancellation is a nonpunitive administrative action.

Quick Quiz 4.4

1. **B.** To be subject to time in prison, a sales agent must knowingly have violated the USA. A client who purchased a security in violation of the USA may recover the original purchase price plus costs involved in filing a lawsuit. In addition, the purchaser is entitled to interest at a rate stated by the Administrator, less any earnings already received on the investment. The right of rescission must be accepted or rejected within 30 days of receipt of the letter of rescission. Although any person aggrieved by an order of the Administrator may request an appeal of the order within 60 days, such appeal does not function as a stay order during the appeal process. The person who is the subject of the order must comply with the order during the period unless a stay is granted by the court.

Appendix A

The NASAA Statement of Policy on Dishonest or Unethical Business Practices of Broker/Dealers and Agents

Adopted May 23, 1983

HIGH STANDARDS AND JUST PRINCIPLES. Each broker/dealer and agent shall observe high standards of commercial honor and just and equitable principles of trade in the conduct of their business. Acts and practices, including but not limited to the following, are considered contrary to such standards and may constitute grounds for denial, suspension or revocation of registration or such other action authorized by statute.

1. Broker/Dealers

    a. Engaging in a pattern of unreasonable and unjustifiable delays in the delivery of securities purchased by any of its customers and/or in the payment upon request of free credit balances reflecting completed transactions of any of its customers.

    b. Inducing trading in a customer's account which is excessive in size or frequency in view of the financial resources and character of the account.

    c. Recommending to a customer the purchase, sale or exchange of any security without reasonable grounds to believe that such transaction or recommendation is suitable for the customer based upon reasonable inquiry concerning the customer's investment objectives, financial situation and needs, and any other relevant information known by the broker/dealer.

d. Executing a transaction on behalf of a customer without authorization to do so.

e. Exercising any discretionary power in effecting a transaction for a customer's account without first obtaining written discretionary authority from the customer, unless the discretionary power relates solely to the time and/or price for the executing of orders.

f. Executing any transaction in a margin account without securing from the customer a properly executed written margin agreement promptly after the initial transaction in the account.

g. Failing to segregate customers' free securities or securities held in safekeeping.

h. Hypothecating a customer's securities without having a lien thereon unless the broker/dealer secures from the customer a properly executed written consent promptly after the initial transaction, except as permitted by Rules of the Securities and Exchange Commission.

i. Entering into a transaction with or for a customer at a price not reasonably related to the current market price of the security or receiving an unreasonable commission or profit.

j. Failing to furnish to a customer purchasing securities in an offering, no later than the due date of confirmation of the transaction, either a final prospectus or a preliminary prospectus and an additional document, which together include all information set forth in the final prospectus.

k. Charging unreasonable and inequitable fees for services performed, including miscellaneous services such as collection of monies due for principal, dividends or interest, exchange or transfer of securities, appraisals, safekeeping, or custody of securities and other services related to its securities business.

l. Offering to buy from or sell to any person any security at a stated price unless such broker/dealer is prepared to purchase or sell, as the case may be, at such price and under such conditions as are stated at the time of such offer to buy or sell.

m. Representing that a security is being offered to a customer "at the market" or a price relevant to the market price unless such broker/dealer knows or has reasonable grounds to believe that a market for such security exists other than that made, created or controlled by such broker/dealer, or by any such person for whom he is acting or with whom he is associated in such distribution, or any person controlled by, controlling or under common control with such broker/dealer.

n. Effecting any transaction in, or inducing the purchase or sale of, any security by means of any manipulative, deceptive or fraudulent device, practice, plan, program, design or contrivance, which may include but not be limited to:

(1) Effecting any transaction in a security which involves no change in the beneficial ownership thereof;

(2) Entering an order or orders for the purchase or sale of any security with the knowledge that an order or orders of substantially the same size, at substantially the same time and substantially the same price, for the sale of any such security, has been or will be entered by or for the same or different parties for the purpose of creating a false or misleading appearance of active trading in the security or a false or misleading appearance with respect to the market for the security; provided, however, nothing in this subsection shall prohibit a broker/dealer from entering bona fide agency cross transactions for its customers; or

(3) Effecting, alone or with one or more other persons, a series of transactions in any security creating actual or apparent active trading in such security or raising or depressing the price of such security, for the purpose of inducing the purchase or sale of such security by others.

o. Guaranteeing a customer against loss in any securities account of such customer carried by the broker/dealer or in any securities transaction effected by the broker/dealer or in any securities transaction effected by the broker/dealer with or for such customer.

p. Publishing or circulating, or causing to be published or circulated, any notice, circular, advertisement, newspaper article, investment service, or communication of any kind which purports to report any transaction as a purchase or sale of any security unless such broker/dealer believes that such transaction was a bona fide purchase or sale or such security; or which purports to quote the bid price or asked price for any security, unless such broker/dealer believes that such quotation represents a bona fide bid for, or offer of, such security.

q. Using any advertising or sales presentation in such a fashion as to be deceptive or misleading. An example of such practice would be a distribution of any nonfactual data, material or presentation based on conjecture, unfounded or unrealistic claims or assertions in any brochure, flyer, or display by words, pictures, graphs or otherwise designed to supplement, detract from, supersede or defeat the purpose or effect of any prospectus or disclosure.

r. Failing to disclose that the broker/dealer is controlled by, controlling, affiliated with or under common control with the issuer of any security before entering into any contract with or for a customer for the purchase or sale of such security, the existence of such control to such customer, and if such disclosure is not made in writing, it shall be supplemented by the giving or sending of written disclosure at or before the completion of the transaction.

s. Failing to make a bona fide public offering of all of the securities allotted to a broker/dealer for distribution, whether acquired as an underwriter, a selling group member, or from a member participating in the distribution as an underwriter or selling group member.

t. Failure or refusal to furnish a customer, upon reasonable request, information to which he is entitled, or to respond to a formal written request or complaint.

2. Agents

a. Engaging in the practice of lending or borrowing money or securities from a customer, or acting as a custodian for money, securities or an executed stock power of a customer.

b. Effecting securities transactions not recorded on the regular books or records of the broker/dealer which the agent represents, unless the transactions are authorized in writing by the broker/dealer prior to execution of the transaction.

c. Establishing or maintaining an account containing fictitious information in order to execute transactions which would otherwise be prohibited.

d. Sharing directly or indirectly in profits or losses in the account of any customer without the written authorization of the customer and the broker/dealer which the agent represents.

e. Dividing or otherwise splitting the agent's commissions, profits or other compensation from the purchase or sale of securities with any person not also registered as an agent for the same broker/dealer, or for a broker/dealer under direct or indirect common control.

f. Engaging in conduct specified in Subsection 1.b, c, d, e, f, i, j, n, o, p, or q.

CONDUCT NOT INCLUSIVE. The conduct set forth above is not inclusive. Engaging in other conduct such as forgery, embezzlement, nondisclosure, incomplete disclosure or misstatement of material facts, or manipulative or deceptive practices shall also be grounds for denial, suspension or revocation of registration.

Appendix B

The NASAA Statement of Policy—Unethical Business Practices of Investment Advisers (with review annotation notes)

The North American Securities Administrators Association has adopted a Statement of Policy on Unethical Business Practices of Investment Advisers. This Statement of Policy is reproduced as follows with review notes included. ■

An investment adviser is a fiduciary and has a duty to act primarily for the benefit of its clients. While the extent and nature of this duty varies according to the nature of the relationship between an investment adviser and its clients and the circumstances of each case, an investment adviser shall not engage in unethical business practices, including the following:

1. Recommending to a client to whom investment supervisory, management, or consulting services are provided the purchase, sale, or exchange of any security without reasonable grounds to believe that the recommendation is suitable for the client on the basis of information furnished by the client after reasonable inquiry concerning the client's investment objectives, financial situation, and needs, and any other information known by the investment adviser.

   Review Note: *An investment adviser providing investment supervisory, management, or consulting services has a fundamental obligation to analyze a client's financial situation and needs prior to making any recommendation to the client. Recommendations made to a client must be reasonable in relation to the information that is obtained concerning the client's investment objective, financial situation, and needs, and other information known by the investment adviser. By failing to make reasonable inquiry or by failing to make recommendations that are in line with the financial situation, investment objectives, and character of a client's account, an investment adviser has not met its primary responsibility.*

2. Exercising any discretionary power in placing an order for the purchase or sale of securities for a client without obtaining prior written discretionary authority from the client, unless the discretionary power relates solely to the price at which, or the time when, an order involving a definite amount of a specified security shall be executed, or both.

   Review Note: *This rule pertains only to investment advisers that place orders for client accounts. Prior to placing an order for an account, an investment adviser exercising discretion should have written discretionary authority from the client. In most cases, discretionary authority is granted in an advisory contract or in a separate document executed at the time the contract is executed. The rule permits oral discretionary authority to be used for the initial transactions in a customer's account within the first 10 business days after the date of the first transaction. An investment adviser is not precluded from exercising discretionary power that relates solely to the price or time at which an order involving a specific amount of a security is authorized by a customer because time and price do not constitute discretion.*

3. Inducing trading in a client's account that is excessive in size or frequency in view of the financial resources, investment objectives, and character of the account.

   Review Note: *This rule is intended to prevent an excessive number of securities transactions from being induced by an investment adviser. There are many situations where an investment adviser may receive commissions, or be affiliated with a person that receives commissions, from the securities transactions that are placed by the investment adviser. In view of the fact that an adviser in such situations can directly benefit from the number of securities transactions effected in a client's account, the rule appropriately forbids an excessive number of transaction orders to be induced by an adviser for a customer's account.*

4. Placing an order to purchase or sell a security for the account of a client without authority to do so.

   Review Note: *This rule is not new to either the securities or investment advisory professions. An investment adviser must have authority to place any order for the account of a client. The authority may be obtained from a client orally or in an agreement executed by the client giving the adviser blanket authority.*

5. Placing an order to purchase or sell a security for the account of a client upon instruction of a third party without first having obtained a written third-party trading authorization from the client.

   Review Note: *It is sound business practice for an investment adviser not to place an order for the account of a customer on instruction of a third party without first knowing that the third party has obtained authority from the client for the order. For example, it would be important for an investment adviser to know that an attorney had power of attorney over an estate whose securities the adviser was managing prior to placing any order on instruction of the attorney. Placing orders under such circumstances could result in substantial civil liability, besides being an unethical practice.*

6. Borrowing money or securities from a client unless the client is a broker/dealer, an affiliate of the investment adviser, or financial institution engaged in the business of loaning funds.

   Review Note: *Unless a client of an investment adviser is engaged in the business of loaning money, is an affiliate of the investment adviser, or is an institution that would engage in this type of activity, an investment adviser must not take advantage of its advisory role by borrowing funds from a client. A client provides a substantial amount of confidential information to an investment adviser regarding the client's financial situation and needs. Using that information to an investment adviser's own advantage by borrowing funds is a breach of confidentiality and may create a material conflict of interest that could influence the advice rendered by the adviser to the client.*

7. Loaning money to a client unless the investment adviser is a financial institution engaged in the business of loaning funds or the client is an affiliate of the investment adviser.

   Review Note: *Like borrowing money from a client, loaning funds to a client by an investment adviser should not be an allowable practice unless the investment adviser is a financial institution normally engaged in the business of loaning funds or unless the client is affiliated with the adviser. Loaning funds may influence decisions made for a client's account and puts the investment adviser in a conflict of interest position because the client becomes a debtor of the adviser after a loan is made.*

8. To misrepresent to any advisory client, or prospective advisory client, the qualifications of the investment adviser or any employee of the investment adviser, or to misrepresent the nature of the advisory services being offered or fees to be charged for such service, or to omit to state a material fact necessary to make the statements made regarding qualifications, services or fees, in light of the circumstances under which they are made, not misleading.

Review Note: When an investment adviser offers its services to a prospective client or when providing services to an existing client, the qualifications of the investment adviser or any employee of the investment adviser and the nature of the advisory services and the fees to be charged must be disclosed in such a way as to not mislead. Overstating the qualifications of the investment adviser or disclosing inaccurately the nature of the advisory services to be provided or fees to be charged are not ethical ways to either acquire or retain clients.

9. Providing a report or recommendation to any advisory client prepared by someone other than the adviser without disclosing the fact. (This prohibition does not apply to a situation where the adviser uses published research reports or statistical analyses to render advice or where an adviser orders such a report in the normal course of providing service.)

   Review Note: If an investment adviser provides a report to a client that is prepared by a third party, the adviser has a responsibility to disclose the fact to the client. By entering into an investment advisory agreement, the client relies upon the expertise of the adviser to provide the advisory service. Thus, if the advice is provided by a third party, it is imperative that the adviser disclose this fact to the client so the client is not misled. The prohibition does not apply when an investment adviser gathers and uses research materials prior to making its recommendation to a client.

10. Charging a client an unreasonable advisory fee.

    *Review Note: This rule is intended to prohibit an investment adviser from charging an excessively high advisory fee. **Unreasonable**, as used in this rule, means unreasonable in relation to fees charged by other advisers for similar services. Although no two advisory services are exactly alike, comparisons can be drawn. In those instances where an advisory fee is out of line with fees charged by other advisers providing essentially the same services, an investment adviser should justify the charge. It would be very difficult for a client to compare various advisory services to evaluate those services and the fees charged. This rule will allow state Administrators to research the competitiveness of an adviser's services and fees to make a determination as to whether the fees being charged are unreasonably high.*

11. Failing to disclose to clients in writing, before any advice is rendered, any material conflict of interest relating to the adviser or any of its employees which could reasonably be expected to impair the rendering of unbiased and objective advice including:

    a. Compensation arrangements connected with advisory services to clients which are in addition to compensation from such clients for such services, and

    b. Charging a client an advisory fee for rendering advice when a commission for executing securities transactions pursuant to such advice will be received by the adviser or its employees.

    Review Note: This rule is designed to require disclosure of all material conflicts of interest relating to the adviser or any of its employees that could affect the advice that is rendered. The two examples cited in the rule pertain to compensation arrangements that benefit the adviser and that are connected with advisory services being provided. However, full disclosure of all other material conflicts of interest, such as affiliations between the investment adviser and product suppliers, are also required to be made under the rule.

12. Guaranteeing a client that a specific result will be achieved (gain or no loss) with advice which will be rendered.

    Review Note: *An investment adviser should not guarantee any gain or against loss in connection with advice that is rendered. By doing so, the adviser fails to maintain an arms-length relationship with a client and puts himself in a conflict of interest position by having a direct interest in the outcome of the advice rendered by the adviser.*

13. Publishing, circulating, or distributing any advertisement which does not comply with the Investment Advisers Act of 1940.

    Review Note: *An investment adviser should not publish, circulate, or distribute any advertisement that is inconsistent with federal rules governing the use of advertisements. Rule 206(4)-1 of the Investment Advisers Act of 1940 contains prohibitions against advertisements containing untrue statements of material fact that refer directly or indirectly to any testimonial of any kind, that refer to past specific recommendations of the investment adviser unless certain conditions are met, that represent that a chart or formula or other device being offered can, by itself, be used to determine which securities are to be bought or sold, or that contain a statement that any analysis, report, or service will be furnished free when such is not the case. These prohibitions are fundamental and sound standards that all investment advisers should follow.*

14. Disclosing the identity, affairs, or investments of any client unless required by law to do so, or unless consented to by the client.

    Review Note: *An investment advisory firm has a responsibility to ensure that all information collected from a client be kept confidential. The only exception to the rule should be in instances where the client authorized the release of such information or when the investment advisory firm is required by law to disclose such information.*

15. Taking any action, directly or indirectly, with respect to those securities or funds in which any client has any beneficial interest, where the investment adviser has custody or possession of such securities or funds when the adviser's action is subject to and does not comply with the requirements of the Investment Advisers Act of 1940.

    Review Note: *In instances where an investment adviser has custody or possession of client's funds or securities, it should comply with the regulations under the Investment Advisers Act of 1940 designed to ensure the safekeeping of those securities and funds. The rules under the act specifically provide that securities of clients be segregated and properly marked, that the funds of the clients be deposited in separate bank accounts, that the investment adviser notify each client as to the place and manner in which such funds and securities are being maintained, that an itemized list of all securities and funds in the adviser's possession be sent to the client not less frequently than every three months, and that all such funds and securities be verified annually by actual examination by an independent CPA on a surprise basis. The rule establishes very conservative measures to safeguard each client's funds and securities held by an investment adviser.*

16. Entering into, extending or renewing any investment advisory contract unless such contract is in ***writing*** and discloses, in substance, the services to be provided, the term of the contract, the advisory fee, the formula for computing the fee, the amount of prepaid fee to be returned in the event of contract termination or non-performance, whether the contract grants discretionary power to the adviser and that no assignment of such contract shall be made by the investment adviser without the consent of the other party to the contract.

Review Note: *The purpose of this rule is to ensure that clients have a document to refer to that describes the basic terms of the agreement the client has entered into with an adviser.*

The conduct set forth above is not inclusive. Engaging in other conduct such as non-disclosure, incomplete disclosure, or deceptive practices shall be deemed an unethical business practice.

Appendix C

Summary of the Uniform Securities Act

SECTION I

Definition of Terms

1. **Agent.** The term *agent* means any individual other than a broker/dealer who represents a broker/dealer or issuer in effecting or attempting to effect purchases or sales of securities. However, the term *agent* does not include an individual who represents an issuer in:

   A. effecting transactions in certain securities exempted under the act—for example, US government and municipal securities; Canadian government and other specified foreign securities; securities of US banks, savings institutions, or trust companies; commercial paper with maturities of nine months or less; or investment contracts issued in connection with an employee's stock purchase, savings, pension, profit sharing, or similar benefit plan;

   B. effecting certain transactions exempted under the act—for example, isolated nonissuer transactions, transactions between the issuer and underwriters, or transactions with savings institutions or trust companies; or

   C. effecting transactions with existing employees, partners, or directors of the issuer if no commission or other remuneration is paid or given directly or indirectly for soliciting any person in the state. A partner, officer, or director of a broker/dealer or issuer is an agent only if he effects or attempts to effect securities transactions in the state.

2. **Broker/dealer.** The term *broker/dealer* means any person engaged in the business of effecting transactions in securities for the account of others or for his own account. However, the term *broker/dealer* does not include:

   A. an agent;

   B. an issuer;

   C. a bank, savings institution, or trust company; or

   D. a person who has no place of business in the state if:

      1) he effects transactions in the state exclusively with or through

         a) the issuers of the securities involved in the transactions,

         b) other broker/dealers, or

         c) banks, savings institutions, trust companies, insurance companies, investment companies (as defined in the Investment Company Act of 1940), pension or profit-sharing trusts, or other financial institutions or institutional buyers, whether acting for themselves or as trustees; or

      2) the person is licensed properly in the state in which the firm maintains a place of business (not in this state) and the only business the firm does in this state is with an existing customer of the firm who is not a resident in this state.

3. **Investment adviser**

   A. The term *investment adviser* means any person:

      1) who, for compensation, engages in the business of advising others, either directly or through publications or writings, as to the value of securities or as to the advisability of investing in, purchasing, or selling securities; or

      2) who, for compensation and as part of a regular business, issues or promulgates analyses or reports concerning securities.

   B. However, the term *investment adviser* does not include the following:

      1) **Institutions.** A bank, savings institution, or trust company.

      2) **Professionals.** A lawyer, accountant, engineer, or teacher whose performance of these services is solely incidental to the practice of his profession.

      3) **Broker/dealers.** A broker/dealer whose performance of these services is solely incidental to the conduct of its business as a broker/dealer and who receives no special compensation for such services.

4) **Publishers.** A publisher of any bona fide newspaper, news magazine, or business or financial publication of general, regular, and paid circulation.

5) **Persons having no place of business in a state.** A person who has no place of business in the state if:

a) such person's only clients in the state are other investment advisers, broker/dealers, banks, savings institutions, trust companies, insurance companies, investment companies (as defined in the Investment Company Act of 1940), pension or profit-sharing trusts, or other financial institutions or institutional buyers, whether acting for themselves or as trustees; or

b) during any period of 12 consecutive months, such person does not direct business communications into the state in any manner to more than five clients other than those specified above, whether or not he or any of the persons to whom the communications are directed are then present in the state.

6) **Persons designated by rule.** Such other persons not within the intent of this definition as the Administrator may, by rule or order, designate.

4. **Issuer.** The term *issuer* means any person who issues or proposes to issue any security.

5. **Security**

A. The term *security* means any:

1) note;

2) stock;

3) treasury stock;

4) bond;

5) debenture;

6) evidence of indebtedness;

7) certificate of interest or participation in any profit-sharing agreement;

8) collateral trust certificate;

9) preorganization certificate or subscription;

10) transferable share;

11) investment contract;

12) voting trust certificate;

13) certificate of deposit for a security;

14) certificate of interest or participation in an oil, gas, or mining title or lease or in payments out of production under such a title or lease; or

15) in general, any interest or instrument commonly known as a security or any certificate of interest or participation in, temporary or interim certificate for, receipt for guarantee of, or warrant or right to subscribe to or purchase any of the foregoing.

B. However, the term *security* does not include:

1) any insurance or endowment policy, or annuity contract under which an insurance company promises to pay a fixed sum of money either in a lump sum or periodically for life or for some other specified period;

2) any interest in a retirement plan such as an IRA, Keogh, or 401(k) plan;

3) collectibles;

4) commodities;

5) condominiums used as a personal residence or business location; or

6) currency.

Comment: *The proper determination of what is or is not a security is crucial to broker/dealers, investment advisers, or agents properly conducting their activities in compliance with state securities laws. Many questions have been raised relating to what constitutes a security. For the most part, these questions have involved special types of investment instruments that are not in the form of stocks, notes, or other traditional securities.*

Investment contracts. *Chief among the types of interests that have been held in certain circumstances to be securities are arrangements known as investment contracts. As established by the federal courts, the basic test for determining whether a specific investment is included in the definition of security is whether the person invests his money in a common enterprise and is led to expect profits from the essential managerial efforts of the promoter or a third party. These arrangements may take the form of interests in oil and gas drilling programs, real estate condominiums and cooperatives, farm lands or animals, commodity option contracts, whiskey warehouse receipts, multilevel distributorship arrangements, and merchandising marketing schemes.*

6. **Miscellaneous definitions**

A. **Administrator.** The Uniform Securities Act provides that the Administrator (or such other designated office such as Commission, Commissioner, or Secretary) will administer the act.

B. **Federal covered adviser.** Under the NSMIA, an investment adviser who is registered only with the SEC. Does not register with the states. Generally $30 million or more under management.

C. **Federal covered security.** Under the NSMIA, a security listed on the NYSE, AMEX, Midwest (Chicago), or Nasdaq National (now Global) Market or any security senior to (bond or preferred) or equal to (rights and warrants). Included in the definition are investment companies registered under the Investment Company Act of 1940. These securities are exempt from the registration and advertising filing requirements of the Uniform Securities Act but are not exempt from the antifraud provisions.

D. **Fraud.** The term *fraud* means an intentional effort to deceive someone for profit; not limited to common-law deceit.

E. **Guaranteed.** The term *guaranteed* means guaranteed as to payment of principal, interest, or dividends.

F. **Nonissuer.** The term *nonissuer* means not directly or indirectly for the benefit of the issuer.

G. **Offer/Offer to sell.** The terms *offer* and *offer to sell* include every attempt or offer to dispose of, or solicitation of an offer to buy, a security or interest in a security for value.

H. **Person.** The term *person* means any individual, corporation, partnership, association, joint stock company, or trust where the interests of the beneficiaries are evidenced by a security, an unincorporated organization, a government, or a political subdivision of a government.

SECTION II

Licensing or Registration Requirements for Broker/Dealers, Agents, and Investment Advisers

1. **Licensing/Registration requirements**

   A. **Broker/dealer.** It is unlawful for any person to transact business in the state as a broker/dealer unless registered as a broker/dealer under the act.

   B. **Agent.** It is unlawful for any person to transact business in the state as an agent unless registered under the act. It is also unlawful for any broker/dealer or issuer to employ an agent unless the agent is registered.

   C. **Investment adviser.** It is unlawful for any person to transact business in the state as an investment adviser unless:

      1) he is so registered under this act; or

      2) he has no place of business in this state; and

a) his only clients in this state are investment companies as defined in the Investment Company Act of 1940, other investment advisers, federal covered advisers, broker/dealers, banks, trust companies, savings and loan associations, insurance companies, employee benefit plans with assets of no less than $1 million, and governmental agencies or instrumentalities, whether acting for themselves or as trustees with investment control, or other institutional investors as are designated by rule or order of the (Administrator), or

b) during any period of the preceding 12 consecutive months, he does not direct business communications in this state in any manner, has had no more than five clients other than those specified in subparagraph a above, whether or not he or any of the persons to whom the communications are directed is then present in this state.

2. **Licensing/Registration applications.** A broker/dealer, agent, or investment adviser may obtain an initial registration by filing with the Administrator an application together with a consent to service of process.

   Comment: *All states prescribe filing and/or examination fees in connection with the filing of an application for registration; those fees vary in amount from state to state.*

3. **Licensing/Registration standards**

   A. **Broker/dealer**

   1) **Minimum capital.** The Administrator may require that the broker/dealer have a minimum net capital as a condition of registration.

   2) **Surety bond.** The Administrator may require registered broker/dealers to post surety bonds in amounts up to $10,000 and may determine their conditions.

   3) **Examinations.** The Administrator may provide for a qualification examination that may be written or oral or both. Depending on the state, the examination may be required to be taken by one or more officers or executive officers of the broker/dealer.

   B. **Agent**

   1) **Surety bond.** The Administrator may require registered agents to post surety bonds in amounts up to $10,000 and may determine their conditions. An appropriate deposit of cash or securities must be accepted instead of a bond.

   2) **Examinations.** The Administrator may provide for a qualification examination that may be written or oral or both.

3) **Notification requirements on termination of relationship.** When an agent begins or terminates a connection with a broker/dealer or issuer, or begins or terminates activities that make him an agent, the agent as well as the broker/dealer or issuer must promptly notify the Administrator.

C. **Investment adviser**

1) **Minimum net worth.** The Administrator may require a minimum networth for registered investment advisers.

2) **Surety bond.** The Administrator may require registered investment advisers to post surety bonds in amounts up to $35,000 and may determine their conditions.

3) **Examinations.** The Administrator may provide for a qualification examination that may be written or oral or both. Depending on the state, an examination may be required to be taken by one or more officers, executive officers, and/or investment counselors actually managing client accounts for clients who reside in the state.

D. **Investment adviser representative**

1) **Examinations.** The Administrator may provide for a qualification examination that may be written or oral or both.

2) **Notification requirements of termination of relationship.** When an investment adviser representative associated with a state covered investment adviser begins or terminates that association, the investment adviser must promptly notify the Administrator. If the investment adviser representative is associated with a federal covered investment adviser, it is the responsibility of the investment adviser representative to promptly notify the Administrator of any change in association.

4. **Term of license/registration.** Every broker/dealer, agent, investment adviser, and investment adviser representative registration expires on December 31 unless renewed on an annual basis.

5. **Post-licensing/registration provisions**

A. **Filing of sales and advertising literature.** The Administrator may require the filing of any prospectus, pamphlet, circular, form letter advertisement, or other sales literature or advertising communication addressed or intended for distribution to prospective investors, including clients to or prospective clients of an investment adviser, unless the security or transaction is exempted under the act.

B. **Recordkeeping requirements.** Every registered broker/dealer and investment adviser must make and keep such accounts, correspondence, memoranda, papers, books, and other records as the Administrator by rule prescribes. (Compliance with the requirements of the SEC concerning preservation of records satisfies most states' recordkeeping requirements.)

C. **Financial reports.** Every registered broker/dealer and investment adviser must file such financial reports as the Administrator prescribes.

D. **Requirement to update information.** If the information contained in any document filed with the Administrator (such as a registered application) is or becomes inaccurate or incomplete in any material respect, the registrant must promptly file a corrective amendment.

E. **Authority of Administrator to conduct examinations.** All records of a broker/dealer or investment adviser are subject at any time, or from time to time, to such reasonable periodic, special, or other examination by representatives of the Administrator, within or outside the state, as the Administrator deems necessary or appropriate in the public interest or for the protection of investors.

SECTION III

Registration of Securities; Exempt Securities and Exempt Transactions

1. **Registration requirement.** It is unlawful for any person to offer or sell any security in this state unless:

   A. it is registered under this act; or

   B. the security or transaction is exempt.

2. **Types of securities registrations**

   A. **Registration by notification or filing.** Registration by notification is generally available for securities of companies that have achieved a specified level of earnings for the past three years. Notification is accomplished by filing with the Administrator a statement demonstrating eligibility to proceed by way of notification and describing the terms of the offering and the names of the underwriters, together with a copy of the offering circular or prospectus to be used.

   B. **Registration by coordination.** An application to register securities by coordination may be filed for any security for which there is a currently pending application to register with the SEC under the Securities Act of 1933. Registration by coordination is effected by filing with the Administrator a registration statement containing a copy of the prospectus as filed under the Securities Act of 1933, the amount of the securities to be offered in the state, and a list of the other states in which the offering will be filed. The registration statement on file with the Administrator becomes effective at the same time as the federal registration, provided no stop order has been issued by the Administrator denying the registration. Any post-effective amendment to the federal registration must also be filed with the Administrator.

C. **Registration by qualification.** Any security may be registered by qualification by filing with the Administrator a registration statement containing specified information about the issuer, including a recent balance sheet and a copy of the proposed offering circular. Securities will be registered by qualification when there is to be no registration of the securities with the SEC or when the SEC registration has already become effective.

D. **Notice filing.** Investment companies registered with the SEC under the Investment Company Act of 1940 are included in the definition of federal covered security. Although exempt from formal registration with the state, they may be required to file a notice with the Administrator, including a consent to service of process, and, possibly, to pay filing fees.

3. **Exempt securities.** The following securities are exempted from the registration and the advertising filing requirements of the act but not from its antifraud provisions:

A. **Governmental securities.** Any security issued or guaranteed by the United States of America, any state or political subdivision, or any agency of the foregoing. Similarly, securities issued by Canada, any provinces thereof, or any other recognized foreign government is also exempt.

B. **Financial institution securities.** Any security issued or guaranteed by, and representing an interest in or debt of, domestic banks, savings and loan associations, or credit unions.

C. **Public utility securities.** These include any security issued or guaranteed by a railroad, other common carriers, public utility, or public utility holding, company regulated in respect to rates by federal or state authority, or regulated in respect to issuance or guarantee of the security by a governmental authority of the United States, any state, Canada, or any Canadian province.

D. **Securities listed on stock exchanges.** Any security listed on the New York or American Stock Exchanges or other approved securities exchanges and any securities equal or senior to such securities. (This exemption had been replaced in some states with a so-called blue-chip exemption that exempts securities of issuers meeting certain financial and operating criteria and is now usurped by the NSMIA with the introduction of the federal covered security.)

E. **Not-for-profit enterprise securities.** Any security issued by a person organized and operated not for profit, but exclusively for religious or charitable purposes.

F. **Commercial paper.** Any commercial paper that evidences an obligation to pay cash within nine months of the date of issuance.

4. **Exempt transactions.** The following transactions are exempted from the registration and the advertising filing requirements of the act but not from its antifraud provision:

    A. **Isolated nonissuer transactions.** Any isolated nonissuer transaction, whether effected through a broker/dealer or not. The term *isolated* is narrowly defined in most states.

    B. **Nonissuer transactions in outstanding securities.** Any nonissuer transaction in an outstanding security (i.e., normal market trading) if:

        1) a recognized securities manual contains the names of the issuer's officers and directors, a balance sheet as of a date within 18 months, and an audited profit and loss statement for the two fiscal years preceding that date; or

        2) the security has a fixed maturity or a fixed interest or dividend provision and there has been no default during the current fiscal year or within the three preceding fiscal years, or during the existence of the issuer and any predecessors if less than three years, in the payment of principal, interest, or dividends on the security.

    C. **Unsolicited transactions.** Any nonissuer transaction effected by or through a registered broker/dealer pursuant to an unsolicited order or offer to buy. The Administrator may require that the customer acknowledge on a specified form that the sale was unsolicited and that a signed copy of each such form be preserved by the broker/dealer for a specified period.

    D. **Fiduciary transactions.** Any transaction by an executor, administrator, sheriff, marshal, receiver, trustee in bankruptcy, guardian, or conservator.

    E. **Transactions with financial institutions.** Any offer or sale to a bank, savings institution, trust company, insurance company, registered investment company, pension or profit-sharing trust, other financial institution or institutional buyer, or broker/dealer, whether the purchaser is acting for itself or as trustee.

    F. **Private placement transactions.** Any transaction, pursuant to an offer directed by the offeror to no more than 10 persons (other than certain financial institutions) in this state during any period of 12 consecutive months, whether or not the offeror or any of the offerees are then present in the state, if:

        1) the seller reasonably believes that all the buyers in the state (other than certain financial institutions) are purchasing for investment; and

        2) no commission or other remuneration is paid or given directly or indirectly for soliciting any prospective buyer in the state (other than financial institutions).

Comment: **Private placement transactions.** *There are important differences between federal and state law with respect to private placements. Under the Securities Act of 1933 and Regulation D promulgated thereunder, there is an exemption from federal registration for private placements that meet prescribed tests relating to the wealth and sophistication of the investors, their access to information concerning the issuer, the manner in which the offering is made, and the number of purchasers. On the other hand, the Uniform Securities Act's private placement exemption is based primarily on the making of a limited number of offers (10) to persons in the state within a period of 12 consecutive months and the nonpayment of sales commissions.*

Thus, the Uniform Securities Act exemption is both broader and narrower than the comparable federal exemption. It is broader in that up to 10 offers and sales may be made in each state, there are no special suitability requirements for offerees, and no requirements that the offerees have access to prescribed information, but it is narrower in that only a limited number of offers may be made and no commissions may be paid.

SECTION IV

Fraudulent and Other Prohibited Business Practices

1. **Sales and purchases.** It is unlawful for any person, in connection with the offer, sale, or purchase of any security, directly or indirectly, to:

   A. employ any device, scheme, or artifice to defraud;

   B. make any untrue statement of a material fact or omit a material fact necessary to make the statements made, in light of the circumstances under which they were made, not misleading; or

   C. engage in any act, practice, or course of business that operates or would operate as a fraud or deceit upon any person.

2. **Advisory activities.**

   A. It is unlawful for any person who receives consideration from another person primarily for advising the other person as to the value of securities or their purchase or sale, whether through the issuance of analyses or reports or otherwise, to:

      1) employ any device, scheme, or artifice to defraud the other person; or

      2) engage in any act, practice, or course of business that operates or would operate as a fraud or deceit upon the other person.

   B. It is unlawful for any investment adviser to enter into, extend, or renew an investment advisory contract unless it provides the following in writing:

1) **No sharing in profits.** That the investment adviser will not be compensated on the basis of a share of capital gains upon or capital appreciation of the funds or any portion of the funds of the client.

2) **No assignment without consent.** That no assignment of the contract may be made by the investment adviser without the consent of the other party to the contract.

3) **Notification of management changes.** That the investment adviser, if a partnership, will notify the other party to the contract of any change in the membership of the partnership within a reasonable amount of time after the change.

C. It is unlawful for any investment adviser to take or have custody of any securities or funds of any client if:

1) the Administrator, by rule, prohibits custody; or

2) in the absence of a rule, the investment adviser fails to notify the Administrator that he has or may have custody.

3. **Prohibited business practices.** State securities laws prohibit agents from engaging in dishonest or unethical business practices or from taking unfair advantage of clients. These prohibitions, which may or may not be specifically defined in a particular state's blue-sky law, apply to offers or sales to investors or purchases from investors.

Although some forms of dishonest or unethical practices are easy to identify, many are not. Generally, each agent, relying on his own common sense and integrity, should be able to determine whether his business practices are dishonest or unethical or whether he is taking unfair advantage of a client.

Set forth below are many, but certainly not all, of the acts that have been committed by agents that have been held to constitute fraudulent, dishonest, or unethical business practices or take unfair advantage of clients:

A. **Misleading or untrue statements.** An agent may not make any misleading or untrue statements of material fact in connection with either the purchase or sale of a security. For example, the following could be untrue statements of a material fact:

1) Inaccurate market quotations

2) Incorrect statements of an issuer's earnings or projected earnings

3) Inaccurate statements about the amount of commission or mark-up/markdown to be charged for effecting a transaction

4) Telling customers that exchange listing of a security is anticipated, without knowledge of the truth of such a statement

5) Telling a customer that a security registered with the SEC or a state securities Administrator has been approved by such regulators

B. **Failure to state important facts.** An agent may not omit a material fact necessary to make his statements not misleading in light of the surrounding circumstances. This means that agents may not be deliberately selective in what they choose to tell a customer.

C. **Inside information.** An agent may not make recommendations on the basis of material inside information about an issuer or its securities when that information has not been made public.

D. **Suitability of recommendations to and transactions for customers**

   1) Failing to make reasonable inquiry of customers regarding their financial situations and needs and investment objectives

   2) Recommending securities transactions to customers without regard to their financial situation or needs or investment objectives

   3) Recommending the purchase or sale of a security without reasonable grounds for the recommendation

   4) Churning customer accounts (i.e., inducing transactions solely to generate commissions without regard to customers' best interests)

   5) Inducing transactions in customer accounts that are excessive in size in view of the customers' financial resources

   6) Failing to sufficiently describe the important facts and risks concerning a transaction or set of transactions

E. **Other prohibited business practices**

   1) Accepting orders on behalf of customers from persons other than the customers without first obtaining written third-power trading authority

   2) Borrowing money or securities from a customer

   3) Commingling (mixing) customers' funds with the agent's own funds

   4) Deliberately failing to follow a customer's instructions

   5) Effecting transactions for or on behalf of customers without specific authority to do so

   6) Effecting transactions with a customer not recorded on the regular books or records of the agent's employing broker/dealer, unless the transactions are disclosed to, and authorized in writing by, the broker/dealer before execution of the transactions

   7) Exercising discretionary authority in a customer's account without first obtaining written discretionary authority from the customer

   8) Failing to bring customers' written complaints to the attention of the agent's employing broker/dealer

9) Failing to inform a customer that certain transactions will involve larger than ordinary commissions, taxes, or transaction costs

10) Guaranteeing customers a profit or a specific result, or guaranteeing against loss

11) Misrepresenting to customers the status of their accounts

12) Participating in activities or transactions that constitute market manipulation, such as phony market quotations, wash sales, matched purchases or sales, and other transactions that may reasonably be expected to distort the trading in a security

13) Participating in transactions that create the misleading appearance of active trading in a security

14) Promising to perform certain services on a customer's behalf, without any intent to perform such services or without being properly qualified to perform such services

15) Sharing in the profits or losses in customer accounts without the written consent of the customer and the agent's employing broker/dealer and not in relationship to the agent's personal funds invested in the account

16) Soliciting orders for unregistered nonexempt securities

17) Representing that the Administrator approves of the broker/dealer's or agent's abilities

SECTION V

Regulatory Oversight, Criminal Penalties, Civil Liabilities: Scope of the Act and General Provisions

1. Regulatory oversight

   A. **Authority to deny, suspend, or revoke registrations**

      1) **Broker/dealers, investment advisers, agents, and investment adviser representatives.** An Administrator may, by order, deny, suspend, or revoke any registration (whether as a broker/dealer, agent, investment adviser, or investment adviser representative) if he finds that the order is in the public interest and that the applicant, registrant, or any partner, officer, director, person occupying a similar status or performing similar functions, person directly or indirectly controlling the broker/dealer, or investment adviser does any of the following or has any of the following issues:

a) **Misleading application.** Has filed an application that is materially incomplete or misleading with respect to any material fact.

b) **Willful violation of act.** Has willfully violated or willfully failed to comply with any provisions of the act.

c) **Conviction within 10 years.** Has been convicted, within the past 10 years, of any misdemeanor involving a security or any aspect of the securities business, or any felony.

d) **Subject to injunction.** Is permanently or temporarily enjoined by any court of competent jurisdiction from engaging in or continuing any conduct or practice involving any aspect of the securities business.

e) **Subject to suspension or revocation.** Is the subject of an order of the Administrator denying, suspending, or revoking registration as a broker/dealer, agent, or investment adviser.

f) **Suspended or revoked within 10 years.** Is the subject of an order entered within the past 10 years by the Administrator of any state or by the SEC denying or revoking registration as a broker/dealer, agent, or investment adviser.

g) **Guilty of dishonest practices.** Has engaged in dishonest or unethical practices in the securities business.

h) **Insolvent.** Other than an agent or investment adviser representative, is insolvent, either in the sense that his liabilities exceed his assets or in the sense that he cannot meet his obligations as they mature.

i) **Not qualified.** Is not qualified on the basis of factors such as training, experience, or knowledge of the securities business. (An Administrator may not deny, suspend, or revoke a registration solely on the basis of lack of experience.)

2) **Securities.** An Administrator may issue a stop order denying effectiveness to, or suspending or revoking the effectiveness of, any registration statement if he finds that the order is in the public interest and that the following has been done:

a) **Misleading application.** The registration statement is incomplete in any material respect or contains any false or misleading statements.

b) **Convicted of securities crime.** Any officer of the issuer or underwriter has been convicted of a crime involving a security.

c) **Subject to injunction.** The security registered is the subject of an injunction entered by a court or any other federal or state act applicable to the offering.

d) **Fraudulent offering.** The offering would operate as a fraud on purchasers.

      e) **Excessive offering expenses or promoter's fees.** The offering would be made with unreasonable underwriter's compensation, promoter's profits, or options.

    B. **Investigations and subpoenas.** The Administrator may conduct investigations for the purpose of determining whether persons have or are about to violate the act. These investigations may be private or public. The Administrator may, by subpoena, compel persons to testify and/or produce records in connection with investigations. If a person refuses to obey a subpoena, the Administrator may petition the appropriate court for enforcement of it.

    C. **Injunctions.** The Administrator may petition the court to enjoin persons from violating or attempting to violate the act. Upon a proper showing, the court may appoint a receiver for the defendant's assets.

2. **Criminal penalties.** Persons convicted of willful violations of the act may be subject to imprisonment and/or fines for each violation. The maximum penalty is a prison term of three years and/or a fine of $5,000.

3. **Civil liabilities.** A person who offers or sells a security in violation of certain provisions of the act is, upon tender of the security, liable to the person purchasing such security for the consideration paid for the security, plus interest at 6% (or the legal rate in most states) per year from the date of the purchase, less the amount of income received on the security by the purchaser, or for damages if the purchaser no longer owns the security. Under blue-sky laws, a person may be held civilly liable for illegal securities transactions for two years from discovery or three years from the date of sale, whichever is sooner.

4. **Scope of the act.** The Scope of the Act section is intended to prescribe the limits of a state's jurisdiction to regulate securities transactions and the activities of persons engaged in the securities business by defining what *in this state* means with respect to:

    A. offers to sell or to buy securities; and

    B. acceptances of offers to buy or sell securities. Generally, the act applies to all offers to buy or sell, and all acceptances of offers to buy or sell, securities if they originate from, are directed to, or are accepted in a state. Any part of an offer that is in this state will subject the whole transaction to the act. Thus, if the client receives a soliciting telephone call in this state, it will not matter that he actually goes out of the state to make payment, sign a contract, or receive the security.

5. **General provisions**

    A. **Misleading filings.** It is unlawful for any person to make or cause to be made, in any document filed with the Administrator or in any proceeding under the act, any statement that is, at the time and in light of the circumstances under which it is made, false or misleading in any material respect.

B. **Rules, forms, orders, and hearings.** The act empowers the Administrator to make, amend, and rescind such rules, forms, and orders and to hold such hearings as are necessary to carry out the provisions of the act. The Administrator may not make a rule, form, or order unless he finds that the action is necessary or appropriate in the public interest or for the protection of investors. In prescribing rules and forms, the Administrator may cooperate with the securities administrators of other states and the SEC to achieve maximum uniformity. All rules and forms of the Administrator must be published.

C. **Administrative files and opinions.** Documents are considered filed under the act when they have been received by the Administrator. Administrators must keep a register of all registrations that have ever been effective under the act and of all denial, suspension, and revocation orders issued. Such register is available for public inspection. Other files made or kept under the act may be made available to the public as the Administrator prescribes by rule. The Administrator, in his discretion, may issue interpretive opinions.

Note: This review of the Uniform Securities Act is a summary of the NASAA study outline.

Glossary

A

accredited investor Any institution or individual meeting minimum net worth requirements for the purchase of securities qualifying under the Regulation D registration exemption, as defined in Rule 501 of Regulation D.

An accredited investor generally is accepted to be one who:

- has a net worth of $1 million or more; or
- has had an annual income of $200,000 or more in each of the two most recent years (or $300,000 jointly with a spouse) and who has a reasonable expectation of reaching the same income level in the current year.

administrator (1) The official or agency administering the securities laws of a state. (2) A person authorized by a court of law to liquidate the estate of an intestate decedent.

advertisement Any material designed for use by newspapers, magazines, radio, television, telephone recording, or any other public medium to solicit business. The firm using advertising has little control over the type of individuals being exposed to the advertising. *See also* sales literature.

affiliate A person in a position to influence the policies of a corporation. This includes partners, officers, directors, and entities who control more than 10% of the voting stock.

agent (1) A securities salesperson who represents a broker/dealer or an issuer when selling or trying to sell securities to the investing public. This individual is considered an agent whether he actually receives or simply solicits orders. (2) A person acting for the accounts of others.

assessable stock Stock issued below par, carrying with it the option on the part of the issuer or creditors to assess the owner for the remainder. A gift of assessable stock is considered a sale under the Uniform Securities Act.

assignment Transferring an investment advisory contract to another firm. This may not be done without written permission from the customer. A change in the majority interest in an investment advisory firm organized as a parntership is also considered assignment.

Any employee, manager, director, officer, or partner of a member broker/dealer or another entity (e.g., issuer, bank) or any person controlling, controlled by, or in common control with that member is considered an associated person of that member.

B

blue sky To qualify a securities offering in a particular state.

blue-sky laws The commonly used term for state regulations governing the securities industry.

brochure rules An investment adviser must provide its customer with its brochure (Part II of Form ADV) at least 48 hours before having him sign the contract. Failing that, the customer must be given five days to void the contract without penalty.

broker The role of a broker/dealer firm when it acts as an agent for a customer and charges the customer a commission for its services.

broker/dealer A firm that acts for the securities accounts of others (acting as a broker) or its own account (acting as a dealer) in trades. Excluded from the definition are:

- agents (registered representatives);
- issuers;
- banks, savings institutions, and trust companies; and
- firms that fit the definition, but (1) have no office in the state and (2) effect transactions only with accredited investors such as issuers, banks, insurance companies, or other broker/dealers, with nonresidents of the state, or with individuals who have fewer than 30 days' residency in the state.

C

cancellation Nonpunitive termination of registration by the Administrator. Reasons include the registrant's death, its ceasing to do business, mental incompetence on the part of the registrant, or the Administrator's inability to locate the registrant.

cease and desist A temporary, or summary, order the Administrator takes to prevent a securities violation. No prior notice or opportunity for a hearing is required for a summary action, but its provisions may not be enforced without a court order. The affected party may demand a hearing in writing within 15 days, and the hearing must take place within 15 days of the Administrator's receipt of the written demand.

churning A prohibited practice in which a salesperson effects transactions in a customer's account that are excessive in size and/or frequency in relation to the size and character of the account.

commingling Mixing broker/dealer or investment adviser cash and securities with customer cash and securities in the same account. This is a prohibited practice.

commission A broker's fee for handling transactions for a client in an agency capacity.

consent to service of process A legal document entered into by all registrants, whereby the Administrator is given the power to accept legal papers on behalf of the registrant.

custodian A commercial bank or trust company that holds monies and securities owned by an investment company in safekeeping.

custody Maintaining possession of a customer's money and/or securities. Many states prohibit investment advisors from keeping custody. The others require the adviser to notify the Administrator if it intends to do so. An adviser is also considered to have custody if the customer has authorized it to receive and disperse funds and securities from his bank account.

D

dealer A firm acting as a principal, for its own account, in a trade. Such a firm actually owns the securities during the trade and charges its customer a markup (if the firm is selling the securities) or a markdown (if the firm is buying them).

debenture An unsecured long-term debt offering by a corporation, promising only the general assets as protection for these creditors.

discretion The authority for someone other than the beneficial owner of an account to make investment decisions for that account regarding the security, the number of shares or units, and whether to buy or sell. Decisions concerning only timing and price do not constitute discretion.

discretionary account An account in which the customer authorizes in writing a broker/dealer or investment adviser to use his judgment in buying and selling securities, including selection, timing, amount, and price. Judgment as to time and/or price only is not considered discretion. Discretionary trades must always be suitable for the customer.

dual registration If a broker/dealer also gives paid investment advice, it must be registered both as a broker/dealer and as an investment adviser. This is known as dual registration. If a broker/dealer gives investment advice only incidentally and is not paid for it, dual registration is not required.

E

effective date The date on which a security can be offered publicly if no stop order is submitted to the issuer by the Administrator.

exempt security A security that need not be in formal compliance with a given piece of legislation, such as the Securities Act of 1933, or the Uniform Securities Act as adopted by a state. Examples are US government and municipal securities. No security is exempt from the antifraud provisions of any securities legislation.

exempt transaction A transaction exempt from registration, sales literature, and advertising requirements under the Uniform Securities Act. Examples of exempt transactions include:

- isolated nonissuer transactions;

- nonissuer transactions in outstanding securities (normal market trading);

- transactions with financial institutions (e.g., banks, savings institutions, trust companies, insurance companies, pension or profit-sharing plans, broker/dealers);

- unsolicited transactions;

- fiduciary transactions;

- private placement transactions;

- transactions between an issuer and its underwriters; and

- transactions with an issuer's employees, partners, or directors if no commission is paid directly or indirectly for the soliciting.

F

federal covered adviser An adviser regulated under the Investment Advisers Act of 1940. A federal covered adviser has a federally imposed exemption from state securities regulation.

federal covered security A security with a federally imposed exemption from state registration. States not only need not register such securities; they are not allowed to. Examples are exchange-listed securities, investment company shares, and Nasdaq National Market securities.

fiduciary A person legally appointed and authorized to represent another person and act on that person's behalf.

foreign government securities Securities issued by the national government of a country with which the United States has diplomatic relations. Such securities are exempt from federal and state registration, but the foreign equivalent of municipal securities is nonexempt.

fraud The deliberate concealment, misrepresentation, or omission of material information or the truth to deceive or manipulate another party for unlawful or unfair gain.

front running Taking action to profit from a customer order before executing the order. Example: if the customer places a large order for a particular stock, the agent might purchase calls on the stock before placing the order and then profit from any price rise caused by the order. This is a prohibited practice.

G

government security An obligation of the US government, backed by the full faith and credit of the government, and regarded as the highest grade or safest issue (i.e., default risk free). The US government issues short-term Treasury bills, medium-term Treasury notes, and long-term Treasury bonds.

guaranteed Securities that have a guarantee, usually from a source other than the issuer, as to the payment of principal, interest, or dividends.

I

inside information Material and nonpublic information a person obtained or used for the purpose of trading in securities. *See also* material fact.

insider Any person who has nonpublic knowledge (material information) about a corporation. Insiders include directors, officers, and stockholders who own more than 10% of any class of equity security of a corporation.

institutional account An account held for the benefit of others. Examples include banks, trusts, pension and profit-sharing plans, mutual funds, and insurance companies.

institutional investor A person or an organization that trades securities in large enough share quantities or dollar amounts that it qualifies for preferential treatment and lower trade costs (commissions). Institutional investors are covered by fewer protective regulations because it is assumed that they are more knowledgeable and better able to protect themselves.

investment adviser Any person who, for compensation (a flat fee or a percentage of assets managed), offers investment advice.

investment adviser representative Any partner, officer, director, or other individual employed by or associated with an investment adviser who (1) gives investment advice or makes recommendations; (2) manages client accounts or portfolios; (3) determines which investment recommendations or advice should be given; (4) offers or sells investment advisory services; or (5) supervises employees involved in any of these activities.

Investment Advisers Act of 1940 Legislation passed by Congress that requires certain investment advisers to register as such with the SEC, to abide by the Investment Advisers Act of 1940 and all other applicable federal acts, and to treat its customers in a fair and equitable manner.

investment company A company engaged primarily in the business of investing and trading in securities, including face-amount certificate companies, unit investment trusts, and management companies.

Investment Company Act of 1940 Congressional legislation enacted to regulate investment companies that requires any investment company in interstate commerce to register with the SEC.

isolated nonissuer transaction An exempt transaction between individual investors, conducted privately. The exempt nature of the transaction must be established by a principal for each separate trade.

issuer (1) The corporation, government, or other entitiy that offers its securities for sale. (2) According to the USA, any person who issues or proposes to issue any security. When a corporation or municipality raises additional capital through an offering of securities, that corporation or municipality is the issuer of those securities.

M

market maker (principal) A dealer willing to accept the risk of holding securities to facilitate trading in a particular security(ies).

matched purchases or sales Simultaneously buying and selling a security to give its trading volume a falsely high appearance. This is a prohibited practice.

material fact Information required to be included in a registration statement that a knowledgeable investor would deem significant in making an investment determination. *See also* inside information.

municipal security Exempt debt security issued by some level of government other than the federal to raise money for a public project. Interest payable on these instruments is not federally taxable.

N

National Conference of Commissioners on Uniform State Laws (NCCUSL) The NCCUSL, founded in 1892, is an organization composed of lawyers who draft and propose template state legislation where uniformity in law among the states is deemed to be desirable. It was the NCCUSL that wrote the Uniform Securities Act. The organization does not, of course, actually write laws, but rather proposes legislation that a state may adopt if it chooses.

National Securities Markets Improvement Act of 1996 Federal legislation designed to clarify the demarcation between federal and state securities law and to improve the efficiency of the securities markets in the United States. Some securities, known as federal covered securities, and some advisory firms, known as federal covered advisers, were removed from state purview to eliminate duplication of regulatory effort.

net capital Liquid capital (cash and assets readily convertible into cash) maintained by a broker/dealer.

nonexempt security A security whose issue and sale must be in compliance with the Uniform Securities Act and/or the various federal securities acts. Most corporate securities are nonexempt.

nonissuer A person other than the issuer of a security. In a nonissuer securities transaction, for example, the issuer is not one of the parties in the transaction, and the transaction, therefore, is not, according to the law, directly or indirectly for the benefit of the issuer. When the USA refers to a nonissuer transaction, it is referring to a transaction in which the proceeds of the sale go to the selling stockholder. Most nonissuer transactions also are called secondary transactions.

North American Securities Administrators Association (NASAA) The NASAA, founded in Kansas in 1919, is the oldest international investor protection organization. Its current membership is 67 Administrators from the territories, districts, and states of the United States, from Mexico, and from the provinces of Canada. The Series 63 is written by the NASAA and administered by NASD.

notice filing Procedure under the Uniform Securities Act whereby an issuer notifies state securities administrators of federal registration.

NSMIA See National Securities Markets Improvement Act of 1996.

O

offer (1) Under the USA, every attempt to solicit a purchase or sale in a security for value. (2) An indication by an investor, trader, or dealer of a willingness to sell a security or commodity.

P

painting the Tape Spurious trading in a particular security among a group of collaborating investors to give a falsely high appearance of interest in the security. This is a prohibited practice.

person In general, any entity that can be held to a contract: an individual, corporation, trust, government, political subdivision, and unincorporated association are examples.

preorganization certificate Agreement for the future purchase of the stock of a corporation when it is eventually formed. Distribution of preorganization certificates is an exempt transaction, provided certain conditions are met.

private placement The USA's private placement provision allows an exemption from full state registration for a security that is offered in that state to no more than 10 noninstitutional investors within a 12-month period.

prospectus The legal document that must be given to every investor who purchases registered securities in an offering. It describes the details of the company and the particular offering. *Syn.* final prospectus.

R

registered investment company An investment company, such as an open-end management company (mutual fund) or closed-end management company, that is registered with the SEC and exempt from state registration and regulation.

registration by coordination A security is eligible for blue-sky registration by coordination in a state if the issuer files for registration of that security under the Securities Act of 1933 and files duplicates of the registration documents with the state Administrator. The state registration becomes effective at the same time the federal registration statement becomes effective.

registration by qualification A security is eligible for blue-sky registration by qualification in a state if all of the offering is to be sold in a single state or if the security is not eligible for another method of state registration. Net worth and disclosure requirements apply, and registration does not become effective until the Administrator so orders.

registration statement Before nonexempt securities can be offered to the public, they require registration under the Securities Act of 1933. The registration statement must disclose all pertinent information concerning the issuer and the offering. This statement is submitted to the SEC in accordance with the requirements of the 1933 act. If the securities are to be sold in only a single state, by qualification, that state's registration requirements apply.

rescission Buying back, from the customer, a security that was inadvertently sold unlawfully. The price is generally the customer's purchase price plus the state's legal rate of interest less any income received. The customer has 30 days to accept or reject the offer.

S

sales literature Any written material used to help sell a product and distributed by the firm in a controlled manner. *See also* advertisement.

Securities Act of 1933 The federal legislation requiring the full and fair disclosure of all material information about the issuance of new securities.

Securities and Exchange Commission (SEC) The commission Congress created to protect investors, which enforces the Securities Act of 1933, the

Securities Exchange Act of 1934, the Investment Company Act of 1940, the Investment Advisers Act of 1940, and other securities laws.

Securities Exchange Act of 1934 The federal legislation establishing the Securities and Exchange Commission that regulates securities exchanges and over-the-counter markets and protects investors from unfair and inequitable practices.

security An investment instrument represented by a certificate or other securitized document, ownership of which yields unpredictable profits or losses that stem from the actions of a third party, usually the issuer of the security. Examples are stocks, bonds, notes, certificates of interest in investment or marketing plans, and options on commodities or on other securities. Whole life insurance, with its table of guaranteed cash values, is not a security, but variable life is. A fixed annuity, with its guaranteed monthly payout, is not a security, but a variable annuity is. A futures contract, with its set terms, is not a security, but an option on that contract is.

self-regulatory organization (SRO) An entity that is accountable to the SEC for the enforcement of federal securities laws, as well as for the supervision of securities practices, within an assigned field of jurisdiction. Examples are NASD, the various stock exchanges, the Municipal Securities Rulemaking Board, and the Chicago Board Options Exchange.

sell The act of conveying ownership of a security or other property for money or other value; every contract to sell a security or an interest in a security. Sales include the following.

- Any security given or delivered with, or as a bonus for, any purchase of securities is considered to have been offered and sold for value.

- A gift of assessable stock is considered to involve an offer and sale.

- Every sale or offer of a warrant or right to purchase or subscribe to another security is considered to include an offer of the other security.

Sales do not include bona fide pledges or loans or stock dividends if nothing of value is given by the stockholders for the dividend.

solicited order An order resulting from a broker/dealer recommendation. The resulting trade must be suitable for the investor.

stop order Action the Administrator takes to prevent an action in the securities market in his state. Unlike cease and desist orders, stop orders require prior notice to the affected party and a hearing with a written finding.

suitable transaction A transaction that meets or takes into account the investment needs of the customer. All solicited transactions must be suitable.

surety bond A bond required for all employees, officers, and partners of member firms to protect clients against acts of misplacement, fraudulent trading, and check forgery.

T

transfer agent A person or an organization responsible for recording the names of registered stockholders and the number of shares owned, seeing that the certificates are signed by the appropriate corporate officers, affixing the corporate seal, and delivering the securities to the transferee.

U

underwriter The entity responsible for marketing stocks, bonds, mutual fund shares, and so forth.

Uniform Securities Act (USA) Template legislation written by the NCCUSL to serve as the basis for a state's securities legislation if it wished to adopt it. It regulates securities, persons (broker/dealers and their agents and investment advisers and their representatives), and transactions in the securities markets within the state. All but a few of the states have adopted the USA in some form.

unsolicited order An order originated by the customer, not the result of a broker/dealer recommendation. The resulting trade is an exempt transaction, though written customer acknowledgment of its unsolicited nature may be required by the Administrator.

unsuitable transaction A transaction that does not meet the investment needs of the customer. An example is purchase of a municipal bond for a low-income customer seeking growth.

W

withdrawal Voluntary termination of registration on the part of the registrant, through submission of Form ADV-W. Withdrawal is effective within 30 days under the Uniform Securities Act unless the Administrator makes a contrary finding.

wrap account An investment advisory account in which all management fees and commissions are combined and paid, usually quarterly, as a fraction of assets under management.

Index

HotSheets

Person

— Individual, company, association, or government

Broker/Dealer Registration

— Must register in state where business is done unless exempt
— Effective after Administrator notification; expires December 31

Exempt from State Registration as a Broker/Dealer

— Banks, savings institutions, other financial institutions, agents, issuers
— Broker/dealers with no office in state only doing business with institutions
— Broker/dealers registered in another state transacting business with a current client passing through a different state

Exemptions from Agent Registration

— Represents issuer in exempt transaction
— Represents issuer in exempt securities
— Represents issuer in sale of employee benefit plans
— Must not receive compensation that is sale related

Agent Registration

— Agents must be registered in state of residence of the client where securities are offered and where securities are sold
— Agents who represent broker/dealers must be registered if they sell exempt or nonexempt securities
— Broker/dealers can only employ registered agents
— Agents who represent issuers generally must be registered if they sell nonexempt securities

— Effective after Administrator notification, no later than noon of the 30th day; expires December 31

— Notification by agent and old and new broker/dealer for employment change

— Notification by state registered investment adviser or investment adviser representative of federal covered adviser for employment change

— Automatic registration of partners, officers, and directors when new broker/dealers and investment advisers register

Investment Adviser Registration

— Federal registered if adviser manages $30 million or more

— State registered if adviser manages less than $25 million

— Choice between federal and state registration if adviser manages at least $25 but not $30 million

— Investment company advisers are always federal registered

— File Form ADV and appropriate fees

— Effective after Administrator notification, no later than noon of the 30th day; expires December 31

Investment Adviser Exemptions

— No office in state and communications directed to 5 or fewer individual residents of the state in 12 months (de minimis)

— No office in state and clients are institutions, broker/dealers, or investment advisers only

Investment Adviser Recordkeeping

— All specific customer and investment adviser records kept for 5 years; must be kept in investment adviser's office for the first 2 years

Broker/Dealer Recordkeeping

— Same as investment adviser except 3 years instead of 5 years

STATE REGISTRATION OF SECURITIES HOTSHEET

Security (Howey Decision)

— Investment of money

— Common enterprise

— Expectation of profits

— Solely from efforts of others

Nonexempt Security

— Must register

Issuer

— Company, government, or government subdivision that offers or proposes to offer securities

Nonissuer

— Secondary market transaction

— Proceeds do not go to issuer

Primary Offering

— Initial public offering and any subsequent offering of new securities

Methods of Registration

— Coordination, qualification

Notice Filing

— Federal covered investment company securities—file documents with states

Exempt Security

— No registration under USA required

— Depends on who the issuer is

— Still subject to antifraud provisions

Exempt Transaction

— Transaction need not be registered under USA

— Depends on who the purchaser is or how the trade is made

HotSheets

UNETHICAL BUSINESS PRACTICES HOTSHEET

Practices Prohibited of All Securities Professionals

— Misleading or untrue statements

— Failure to state material facts

— Use of insider information

— Unsuitable transactions

— Market manipulation (pegging, front running, wash sales, matched purchases)

Other Prohibited Sales Practices

— Unauthorized third-party trading

— Borrowing money from customers who are not banks, broker/dealers, or lending institutions

— Lending money to customers unless the firm is in the money lending business

— Commingling client funds with funds of the agent or the firm

— Failing to follow client instructions

— Exercising discretion without written authority

— Effecting transactions not on the books (selling away)

— Failing to report written complaints

— Guaranteeing against loss

— Failing to inform clients of higher than normal charges

— Misrepresenting customer account status

— Creating misleading trading activity

— Promising undeliverable services

— Unauthorized sharing in customer accounts

— Solicitation of unregistered, nonexempt securities

— Misrepresenting Administrator approval

Unlawful or Unethical Investment Advisory Practices

— Unsuitable investments

— Unauthorized discretion

— Unauthorized third-party transactions

— Excessive trading

— Commingling of funds

— Misrepresentation of material facts

— Nondisclosure of information sources

— Excessive fees

— Conflicts of interest

— Unauthorized custody of customer funds

— Operating without advisory contracts

— Performance-based compensation, unless legally permitted

— Failing to disclose material legal action in past 10 years at least 48 hours before contracting with client

— Failing to disclose principal or agent capacity

— Assignment of an advisory contract without client consent

HotSheets

USA as Model Legislation

— USA is not actual but model legislation for each state's own legislation

NSMIA of 1996

— Eliminates state and federal registration duplication

Federal Covered Securities

— Covered by national, not state, regulation

— Includes securities listed on US exchanges and Nasdaq National Market (not SmallCap), issued by investment companies, or private placements

— Includes government and municipal bonds (but not municipal bonds issued within that state)

Administrator

— State official responsible for implementation of the USA

Powers of the Administrator

— Make rules and orders

— Conduct investigations and issue subpoenas

— Issue cease and desist orders and seek injunctions

— Deny, suspend, cancel, or revoke registrations

Fraud

— Willful misrepresentation for unlawful gain

Civil Liabilities

— Attorney's costs plus losses on investment plus interest minus any income received

Rescission

— Right to rescind a transaction in violation of the USA—30-day letter

Criminal Penalties

— Fines, imprisonment, or both

Statute of Limitations

— Time limits for bringing suit in a case
— Civil—3 years from date of sale or rendering of advice or 2 years after discovering violation, whichever occurs first
— Criminal—5 years after date of transaction